Will Ferrell

Titles in the People in the News series include:

Tim Allen	Dominique Moceanu
Drew Barrymore	Rosie O'Donnell
Tony Blair	Mary-Kate and Ashley Olsen
Bono	The Osbournes
Garth Brooks	Brad Pitt
Sandra Bullock	Colin Powell
George W. Bush	Princess Diana
Nicolas Cage	Prince William
Jim Carrey	Christopher Reeve
Michael Crichton	Julia Roberts
Tom Cruise	The Rolling Stones
Matt Damon	J.K. Rowling
Johnny Depp	Adam Sandler
Celine Dion	Arnold Schwarzenegger
Eminem	Will Smith
Michael J. Fox	Britney Spears
Bill Gates	Steven Spielberg
Mel Gibson	R.L. Stine
John Grisham	Sting
Tom Hanks	John Travolta
Jesse Jackson	Jesse Ventura
Michael Jackson	Robin Williams
Michael Jordan	Oprah Winfrey
Stephen King	Reese Witherspoon
Jennifer Lopez	Elijah Wood
George Lucas	Tiger Woods
Madonna	

PEOPLE
IN THE NEWS

Will Ferrell

by Dwayne Epstein

LUCENT BOOKS
An imprint of Thomson Gale, a part of The Thomson Corporation

Detroit • New York • San Francisco • San Diego • New Haven, Conn.
Waterville, Maine • London • Munich

THOMSON

━━━━━━✦━━━━━━ ™

GALE

LIBRARY OF CONGRESS CATALOGING-IN-PUBLICATION DATA

Epstein, Dwayne.
Will Ferrell / by Dwayne Epstein.
p. cm. — (People in the news)
Includes bibliographical references and index.
ISBN 1-59018-716-4 (hard cover : alk. paper)
1. Ferrell, Will, 1967—Juvenile literature. 2. Actors—United States—Biography—Juvenile literature. I. Title. II. Series: People in the news (San Diego, Calif.)
PN2287.F42E68 2005
792.702'8'092—dc22   2004030914

Printed in the United States of America

Table of Contents

Foreword

FAME AND CELEBRITY are alluring. People are drawn to those who walk in fame's spotlight, whether they are known for great accomplishments or for notorious deeds. The lives of the famous pique public interest and attract attention, perhaps because their experiences seem in some ways so different from, yet in other ways so similar to, our own.

Newspapers, magazines, and television regularly capitalize on this fascination with celebrity by running profiles of famous people. For example, television programs such as *Entertainment Tonight* devote all of their programming to stories about entertainment and entertainers. Magazines such as *People* fill their pages with stories of the private lives of famous people. Even newspapers, newsmagazines, and television news frequently delve into the lives of well-known personalities. Despite the number of articles and programs, few provide more than a superficial glimpse at their subjects.

Lucent's People in the News series offers young readers a deeper look into the lives of today's news makers, the influences that have shaped them, and the impact they have had in their fields of endeavor and on other people's lives. The subjects of the series hail from many disciplines and walks of life. They include authors, musicians, athletes, political leaders, entertainers, entrepreneurs, and others who have made a mark on modern life and who, in many cases, will continue to do so for years to come.

These biographies are more than factual chronicles. Each book emphasizes the contributions, accomplishments, or deeds that have brought fame or notoriety to the individual and shows how that person has influenced modern life. Authors portray their subjects in a realistic, unsentimental light. For example, Bill Gates—the cofounder and chief executive officer of the soft-

6

ware giant Microsoft—has been instrumental in making personal computers the most vital tool of the modern age. Few dispute his business savvy, his perseverance, or his technical expertise, yet critics say he is ruthless in his dealings with competitors and driven more by his desire to maintain Microsoft's dominance in the computer industry than by an interest in furthering technology.

In these books, young readers will encounter inspiring stories about real people who achieved success despite enormous obstacles. Oprah Winfrey—the most powerful, most watched, and wealthiest woman on television today—spent the first six years of her life in the care of her grandparents while her unwed mother sought work and a better life elsewhere. Her adolescence was colored by promiscuity, pregnancy at age fourteen, rape, and sexual abuse.

Each author documents and supports his or her work with an array of primary and secondary source quotations taken from diaries, letters, speeches, and interviews. All quotes are footnoted to show readers exactly how and where biographers derive their information and provide guidance for further research. The quotations enliven the text by giving readers eyewitness views of the life and accomplishments of each person covered in the People in the News series.

In addition, each book in the series includes photographs, annotated bibliographies, timelines, and comprehensive indexes. For both the casual reader and the student researcher, the People in the News series offers insight into the lives of today's news makers—people who shape the way we live, work, and play in the modern age.

Introduction

Outrageous Hubris

*M*ERRIAM-WEBSTER'S COLLEGIATE *Dictionary* defines *hubris* as exaggerated pride or self-confidence. Will Ferrell has become one of the biggest box office stars in America on the basis of a strong comedy persona: He creates characters and situations that reek of hubris, yet are extremely funny.

Pride, overconfidence, and boorishness are generally not laughing matters. Audiences find these human flaws disagreeable and writers find it difficult to depict characters with such superficial, unredeeming traits in any depth. For these reasons, displays of hubris in films and on TV tend to be confined to villains and supporting roles. Ferrell, however, has the singular ability of expressing hubris in funny and appealing ways in leading roles, and his fan base grows with every performance.

Another important aspect of Ferrell's comedy persona is his willingness to go to comedic extremes in performance, in sharp contrast to his handsome, leading-man appearance. Ferrell looks like a typical well-groomed, upper-middle-class dad, but he has no qualms about appearing on a talk show wearing a thong, portraying high-energy characters who scream until they are hoarse, or even squeezing his over-six-foot frame into the tiny costume of his leading character in the film *Elf.*

Ferrell's persona out of the public eye is actually quite different from the characters he often portrays on TV and in films. A basically shy and well-adjusted man, he uses the outrageous characters he inhabits as a concentration device. By blocking out everything around him and convincing himself that it is the character he is playing who is exhibiting the outrageous behavior, he gives himself the freedom to do anything required of him to get a laugh.

Will Ferrell and his wife, Viveca Paulin, arrive at a 2005 awards show. Ferrell is famous for the outrageous characters he has played on television and in film.

Ferrell's impressive ability to portray hubris comedically and to also be utterly outrageous is only part of his appeal. It does not fully explain his lengthy tenure on the sketch-comedy show *Saturday Night Live* (SNL) as one of the most popular cast members in the show's long history, or his starring roles in a string of highly successful films.

His success is due in large part to a personal likeability that comes across in spite of his characters' often dislikable traits. While lesser performers would be playing such roles only in supporting parts, Ferrell manages to draw audiences who cannot seem to get enough of his brand of intense outrageousness and hubris. Ferrell's charismatic personality in lead roles has created a huge personal following that continues to grow as he shows no sign of exhausting his comedic imagination.

One Happy Little Boy

THE EVENTS PEOPLE experience in childhood contribute to the formation of the adult personality. Unlike many talented comedians who use humor to cover the pain of divorce or financial insecurity in their young years, Will Ferrell views his childhood with a positive attitude. This attitude would not only bring joy to the people closest to him throughout his life but would prove to be the foundation of his sense of humor.

Musical Roots

Will's parents, Lee and Kay Ferrell, both grew up in North Carolina but migrated to Southern California in the early 1960s to promote Lee's fledgling musical career. Lee was quite adept at many instruments, including the saxophone and various keyboards. After arriving in California, Lee eventually found work playing with Dick Dale, known as "the King of the Surf Guitar." Dale and his band, the Del Tones, were featured in the 1964 film *Muscle Beach Party*; Lee Ferrell can be seen in the background playing the saxophone.

Since the income of a musician is often sporadic at best, Kay Ferrell began teaching English at Santa Ana Community College. The Ferrells moved to Irvine, and when Lee found permanent work in 1967 providing keyboards, saxophone, and background vocals for the popular singing duo the Righteous Brothers, the couple settled into raising a family.

Life in a Bedroom Community

John William Ferrell was born on July 16, 1967, in Irvine. He was the first of two sons; his brother, Patrick, was born less than two years later. Nestled in the heart of conservative Orange County, Irvine boasted a fairly affluent middle-class existence. The Ferrells lived in the Park West apartment complex, one of only two such complexes in the entire city at the time. Since both the older Ferrells worked, the family's situation was unusual in the community. Most of Irvine's population consisted of upper-middle-class families in which the father practiced a profession and the mother stayed at home tending the children. "It's a real bedroom community [that is, a quiet neighborhood]," Will would later say.

In 1967 Lee Ferrell, an aspiring musician, began performing with the Righteous Brothers (pictured). The steady income from these gigs allowed him to start a family.

This aerial view shows the coastline of Orange County. Will was raised in Irvine, a city in the heart of Orange County.

"There's not a lot of gang warfare in Irvine. Couple that with a happy home life and I'm not your typical artist. I'm too content and laid back to be a tortured soul."[1]

Will's hometown of Irvine has gone through much growth since it was first incorporated in 1971. Located in the heart of Orange County, just forty miles south of Los Angeles, Irvine consists of fifty-five square miles situated between fashionable Costa Mesa to the south, Riverside to the east, and the less affluent Santa Ana to the north. The weather in the planned community of mostly newer homes and businesses is a fairly constant 71°F most of the year, which might explain the next statistic: The city's population was a little over 14,000 in 1971, but during Will's childhood mushroomed to over 171,000. That gigantic growth rate has since tapered off considerably. The presence of UC Irvine, part of the highly regarded University of California system, also played an important role in the community's growth.

In spite of its growth, certain aspects of Irvine have not changed much since Will was young. Then, as now, the population was mostly Caucasian, with a small number of Asians, Hispanics, and African Americans combined totaling less than 40 percent of the population. Republican voters still outnumber Democrats two to one, the median age is still thirty-nine, and the typical income is slightly higher than the national average. In essence, the community of Irvine remains the typical Orange County community.

Will spent his early years in Irvine like most children, playing with his beloved Matchbox cars and Tonka trucks. The sandy-haired youngster amazed his parents with his sweet disposition. "He was born like that, very even tempered, very easy-going," recalls his mother. "His father and I kind of went, 'How'd he get like that?' . . . Will would line up his Matchbox cars, by himself, and be totally happy. You'd say, 'You want to go to Disneyland today or line up your cars?' and he'd have to think about it."[2]

Two Christmases in One

By the time Will started school, problems had begun to surface in his parents' marriage. One problem may have been the instability of his father's work. When the Righteous Brothers toured, Lee Ferrell was gone for months at a time, and between recordings his income was anything but steady. In 1975, when Will was eight years old, his parents divorced, but they remained friends. Kay Ferrell kept working at nearby Santa Ana Community College and Lee moved out of the apartment, staying close enough to help Kay raise their two sons. Will's mother would later say that she and her ex-husband had a much better divorce than they did a marriage.

In spite of the divorce, the Ferrells kept the well-being of Will and Patrick a top priority throughout the boys' formative years. This support, coupled with an easygoing disposition, contributed to Will's ability to maintain a positive attitude. "I was the type of kid," he says, "who would say, 'Look at the bright side! We'll have two Christmases.'"[3]

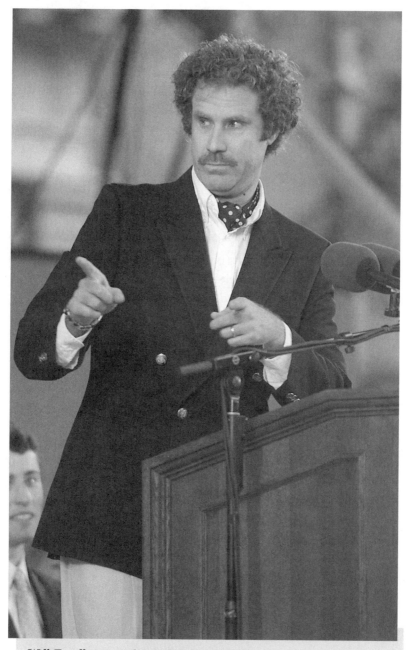

Will Ferrell gives students a laugh as he delivers the commencement speech to the 2003 graduating class of Harvard University. Will discovered his comic talents as a young boy.

Following his parents' divorce, Will and his brother lived with both parents periodically. A good deal of Will's childhood was also spent visiting his grandmother, Katie Overman, in Roanoke Rapids, North Carolina. When Will became a star on *Saturday Night Live*, Grandmother Overman told a local reporter she was surprised at Will's success, saying she felt the boy would never amount to anything. "My grandmother was always suspicious of show business,"[4] says Will.

Conscientious Class Clown

Will attended elementary school in Irvine and was fairly popular with the other students, despite his family's modest lifestyle. Growing up the child of divorced parents also made Will atypical in the upper-middle-class community. Even today, fewer than 11 percent of Irvine's population is divorced. When Will was growing up, that number was significantly smaller.

Lee and Kay Ferrell's ability to maintain an amicable relationship after their breakup went a long way toward keeping Will and Patrick from feeling neglected or traumatized by the divorce. Will was, by most accounts, a happy child who laughed and played with other children and showed an aptitude for sports as well as academics. Over the years, reporters have often asked him if he had a dark, tragic side to his childhood that fueled his need to be funny. He explains, "A lot of people have gotten into comedy because of certain influences in their lives or events that were painful, and I really have wracked my brain to figure it out. I pretty much have had a normal childhood. Maybe it was too normal."[5]

The modest popularity Will enjoyed in grade school was due in part to his naturally sunny outlook, and his ability to be funny endeared him to his peers. In second grade he managed to make the girls in his class giggle by punching himself in the head. By fifth grade his "act" included the occasional pratfall as well as the well-timed bump into a door.

These moments of silliness were sporadic by choice; he made a conscious effort not to overdo his newly discovered ability to make people laugh. He also knew when to act up and when to behave, oftentimes being the one to settle his classmates down once the teacher called the class to order. He says: "I like to characterize myself as a conscientious class clown. I enjoyed being funny and making my friends laugh but I wasn't obnoxious. I never got kicked out of class. I knew when enough was enough."[6]

University High School

Following grade school and a short stint in middle school, Will entered University High School, one of the most prestigious secondary schools in the state. Located in an area of Irvine known as Turtle Rock, it comprises nearly fifty acres of property and was the first high school built in the city. "Uni," as the locals call it, maintains a high academic achievement level and proudly boasts of the athletic prowess of its home team, the Trojans. The overwhelming majority of Uni graduates go on to college, and the school has been nationally recognized several times as an exemplary institute of education.

Will's popularity continued to grow during his years at University High School. He did well in his classes and maintained

Lee Ferrell's Brush with Danger

Will Ferrell's father still lives in Irvine and recently made the local news. However, it was a story he would rather have not been a part of. According to the headline of the March 6, 2003, *Irvine World News* online edition: "A 60-year-old Irvine man was held at gunpoint and tied up in his home with Valentine lights Tuesday by a man who was trying to steal his car."

According to the article by reporter Laylan Connelly, Lee Ferrell was the victim of a carjacking by a thirty-year-old man who was eventually caught by police following a high-speed chase. Ferrell told the newspaper about the ordeal, "I tried to talk him out of it. I said, 'You don't want to do that, you better take the car and leave.' It was frightening, going in the house with no one around." The armed robber took $300 and stole a 2002 Toyota Avalon out of Ferrell's garage.

Highway patrol officers were able to eventually catch the suspect. "I was really impressed and thankful that the Irvine police force was so efficient and quick, and actually helpful to me," Ferrell said. Interestingly, nowhere in the article is Lee Ferrell identified as the father of Will Ferrell.

a close coterie of friends—outgoing and well-meaning young men who on occasion committed minor pranks for their own amusement or to get a laugh. They did such things as join a dance class on a lark, since they assumed it would be an easy grade. Once Will and his friends showed up in class dressed in pajamas, just to see if anyone would notice. As a joke Will tried to start a reptile club on campus, but no one showed up with an actual reptile and the club disbanded after only two meetings.

As they had in elementary school, Will and his friends perpetrated these escapades without causing any major disruption in the classroom. They maintained their freedom to commit tomfoolery with an innate knowledge of when to draw the line. This endeared Will to the student body, and he was voted Best Personality by his fellow classmates.

More Jock than Clown

His penchant for the occasional prank aside, Will participated in extracurricular activities and was elected to the student council. One would expect him to have been involved in high school theatrics, but this was not the case. What he excelled at the most in school was sports. By the time he reached his teens he stood six-foot-three, with his younger brother Patrick outdistancing him by two inches. Will was a competitive athlete in soccer, football, and basketball. His high school basketball coach, Steve Scoggin, says of him: "He was like my sixth man off the bench. . . . I would always put him on the other team's best offensive player. And he was also my team captain."[7]

When it came to football, Will made University High School's varsity team and excelled as the team's star field goal kicker. There are countless stories of field goal kickers losing a big game by one point when they broke under pressure. Will learned to use the screaming crowds and the intense pressure of the situation to his advantage, developing a mind-set that would later aid him in his work as a comic actor. "My practice was hours and hours of kicking a football through these goal posts. It was just kind of a Zen-like meditative state,"[8] he explains.

Typical of most teenage boys, Will did not spend all of his time goofing around with his friends and practicing his field goal kick-

As a teen, Will was impressed by the improvisational comedy of, from left, Martin Short, Andrea Martin, and John Candy of the Canadian comedy show, SCTV.

ing. He also took an active interest in girls. He had a serious girlfriend for a while, but the relationship lasted only a few months. He was considered affable and fun-loving, but hardly the type to be taken seriously by the opposite sex. He says, "Girls liked me to be the cafeteria jokester but they didn't want to go out with me on Friday nights."[9] The lack of romance in his teenage years was a disappointment, but his naturally positive outlook helped him keep it in perspective.

Early Influences

It was during his high school years that Will first took notice of professional comedians. No one particular experience determined the career path he would take; rather a serious interest in comedy came only gradually.

Learning the Truth About Santa

When Will Ferrell was doing publicity for the film *Elf* in 2003, film critic Lee Shoquist asked him when he stopped believing in Santa Claus. Ferrell replied:

> I wholeheartedly believed as long as I possibly could. Up until last week actually. And boy, that was tough to get out of bed that day. I don't know when—I was ten, eleven, twelve when I walked into my dad's closet and saw a toy that I knew my brother was getting, and it took my breath away. It was like, "Oh, damn. The rumors I've heard. They're true." But I kept it from my younger brother for as long as I could. But I think my brother was always one step ahead of me, like, "He doesn't exist."

Will was like many casual fans of comedy of the period, who perhaps had a couple of Steve Martin comedy records mixed in with their rock album collection. The impact of comedy on Will in his teen years was largely a matter of staying up late to watch the debut of a new young comic on *The Tonight Show with Johnny Carson*. For example, he says he has a crystallized memory of seeing a little Jerry Seinfeld and Garry Shandling both perform for the first time in the early 1980s, and he took note of the differences between them.

He would later claim that the unique sketch-comedy show known as *Second City Television* (SCTV) had the greatest impact on him. Originating in Canada during the 1980s, the show featured several talented improvisational actors and actresses who created cutting-edge satire under the guise of a fake television network. Within its faux parameters, SCTV parodied movies, culture, show business, and—mostly—television itself in a way that often rivaled its more popular counterpart, *Saturday Night Live*. Most of its cast members, including Martin Short and the late John Candy, went on to have great success, and the show itself maintains a cult status among its fans. Will was one such fan, and he often acted out his favorite moments from recently aired episodes for his high school friends. As he would later state, "I would go from watching *Saturday Night Live* to *The Tonight Show* . . . Those things put together and SCTV collectively influenced me in different kinds of ways."[10]

Senior Year

One of Will's best friends was senior class president, and it was his responsibility to read the morning announcements over the school's public address system. On occasion he asked Will to help him out, and together they devised little skits to liven up the proceedings. When the senior class fund-raiser—a T-shirt sale—had a less-than-enthusiastic response, Will and his friend decided to write and perform a skit for the morning announcements that would jump-start sales. The marketing skit poked gentle fun at several well-known classmates and fictional characters the young writers created. It proved to be not unlike SCTV, but on a much smaller scale. The boys intended the skit to be a one-shot deal, but faculty members soon approached them, asking when they were going to give a repeat performance. Eventually, Will was asked to perform at school assemblies as well.

Plans for the Future

At the end of his senior year, Will had to decide what direction he wanted the rest of his life to take. The public address

An avid sports fan, Will, seen here at a 2004 Lakers basketball game, nearly pursued a career in sports journalism.

announcements and assembly performances had been fun, but he did not see professional comedy as a career option worth pursuing.

He knew he had a likeable personality, and his love of sports was undeniable. This, coupled with his naturally upbeat disposition, led him to look into a career in sports journalism. He discovered that the University of Southern California (USC) offered a program that seemed tailor-made for him, and he decided to enroll.

Will purposely avoided looking into comedy or any other form of show business as a career option. He had witnessed the roller coaster ride his father's show business career had been, and he was determined to avoid it at all costs. "I saw the instability of it," he says. "Even as a little kid, I said I was going to be a businessman."[11]

So in 1986, the little boy who had once believed himself lucky to get two Christmases had become a young man, and prepared to enter USC as a sports information major.

Chapter 2

A Funnyman's Groundwork

T HE REALIZATION THAT he could make a living being funny—and how much he enjoyed doing it—came very slowly to Will Ferrell. No metaphorical lightbulb went off in his head. However, once he overcame his resistance to the idea of following his father into the treacherous realm of show business, he wasted no time laying the groundwork for a transition from sports journalism to comedy.

Trojan Hall

Ferrell would not decide to pursue a career in show business until after he finished college. Sports information is not a very common college major, but it seemed perfectly suited to Ferrell's ambitions. He took the required classes in hopes of landing a job as a sportscaster on the network news or the then-burgeoning arena of cable sports networks. Essentially, the curriculum was that of a journalism major with an added emphasis on sports through such specialized classes as Volleyball and The History of Football.

Ferrell utilized his love of sports and his outgoing personality to the fullest in his attempt to succeed at USC. He managed the class requirements, but spent more time indulging in the college's social life. He lived on the first floor of Trojan Hall and decided to join the international fraternity Delta Tau Delta.

His love of pranks carried over from high school as he and his fraternity brothers indulged themselves to their heart's content. While hanging out with his friends, Ferrell called other dorm rooms pretending to be a material waste expert. His friends laughed hysterically as Ferrell explained in total seriousness that a chemical spill on the 110 freeway required that all students stay in their rooms for the entire day.

His funny side, always spontaneously bubbling to the surface, found a perfect outlet at college. Still stifling the urge to consider pursuing comedy professionally, Ferrell found himself performing anyway. On occasion he would stand outside the cafeteria holding a makeshift megaphone he constructed out of a poster tube and shout at anyone passing by. One such exclamation was: "I repeat, do not eat the fish. The health department has announced . . . "[12]

USC's New Janitor

Ferrell maintained his classes as best as possible but only managed a 2.97 grade point average. This lackluster number translated to a C letter grade and was the direct result of spending too much time doing things other than studying. He had landed a work-study job in the Humanities Audiovisual Department in which he was in charge of checking out overhead projectors and other equipment. Since the job required him to be all over campus, no one really kept track of his whereabouts. If he was not at his post, people assumed he was simply delivering a projector.

This independent routine quickly turned into something else. On occasion Ferrell took it upon himself to visit his friends in class. Knowing he could not simply walk into a classroom without a reason, he slipped on janitor's coveralls. Thus disguised, he could walk into the middle of any class to find a friend.

The class he interrupted the most was a high-level English class called Thematic Option. Ferrell's ability to impersonate a janitor and seem genuinely interested during the lecture proved to be a very successful ruse. While on campus several days later, he was confronted by the professor, who surprised Ferrell by telling him to stop by again in two weeks. "So I would stand outside the door with a power drill and just pretend like I was working on stuff,"[13] recalls Ferrell.

Dressing up as a janitor to sneak into classes was not the only mischief Ferrell perpetrated. He and several friends also managed to indulge in a popular college prank known as streaking. This stunt requires more courage than brainpower: Streakers take off all their clothes and run naked through a predesignated area. The trick is to dash across a heavily populated area of shocked onlookers without being recognized and, more important, without getting caught. Ferrell was apparently quite successful on both counts.

As a student at USC, Ferrell joined a fraternity like this one. He frequently entertained his fraternity brothers by performing hilarious pranks.

Local Intern

In spite of such indulgences, in 1990 Ferrell graduated from USC with a Bachelor of Arts degree in sports information. When asked what exactly the major consisted of, Ferrell responds, "I ask myself that question every day. Let's put it this way: I'm one of the first, and last sports information majors from the University of Southern California."[14] His plan was to put the degree to use by first interning at a local news station and then moving on to one of the networks.

After college, Ferrell became an intern in the sports department at a local news access station, where he learned his craft in a hands-on environment and also managed to get on the air. He quickly found the work to be both unrewarding and uninspiring. He still was not sure what he wanted to do with his life, but he was beginning to get a vague inkling. He often ad-libbed when he was on the air and managed to get a few laughs from the rest of the staff. "Midway through my training," he recalls, "I realized I enjoyed performing for the camera much more than I enjoyed reporting."[15]

Moving On

Realizing that if he stayed at the station he would eventually be locked into a career he disliked, Ferrell moved back in with his mother. Since he also needed an income, he took whatever work was available—and soon found that to be even worse than the job he had left. He worked for a short time parking cars at the Meridien Hotel in Newport Beach. On his second day, he attempted to squeeze a van with an oversized luggage rack into the hotel's parking structure. The entire luggage rack was sheared off, and Ferrell was amazed that he was not fired on the spot.

While living with his mother, Ferrell decided to finally give in to the urge that had been gnawing at him since high school: He tried his hand at performing stand-up comedy. The results were less than spectacular; both the aggressive competition among comedians and the intense pressure to be funny on demand worked against his nature. "I can't tell jokes, really," he says. "I can never remember them. There was a brief time I

Improvisational Theater in America

Will Ferrell's training with the improv troupe the Groundlings proved to be an important foundation for his career in show business. Improv theater in America began when University of Chicago student Paul Sills and several others rented a nightclub and began performing scenes for paying customers in 1955. Sills took what he had learned from his mother—legendary improvisational acting teacher Viola Spolin—out of the classroom and into the realm of professional theater. The company he cofounded eventually evolved into Second City, often considered the premier improvisational theater troupe in America. Many members went on to become influential actors, writers, and directors. Two of its founders, comedians Jerry Stiller and Anne Meara, are the parents of Ben Stiller, Will Ferrell's frequent costar.

San Francisco's the Committee proved to be a popular West Coast offshoot of Second City until its demise in 1973. It was founded by Second City alumni Alan Myerson following a conflict with Paul Sills. The Committee had a direct influence on the Groundlings; one of its members, Gary Austin, began the Los Angeles group as a workshop in 1972. One of its first members was Kip King, father of Will Ferrell's SNL costar, Chris Kattan.

Improvisation has seen many incarnations over time, and its influence can still be felt on such TV shows as SNL and *Mad TV*. Because its roots are in nightclub comedy performances, it has not often been given the same respect as "legitimate" theater productions. However, the talent required to perform something wonderful on the spur of the moment is a rare gift that delights audiences.

did standup. . . . I remember bombing so hard that all the moisture left my mouth and my tongue kept sticking to the roof of my mouth, to the point where it became like a speech impediment thing."[16]

His mother suggested he take some theater classes at Costa Mesa Community College to get a better idea of where his interests might lie. While he was there he met a student named Viveca Paulin. The pretty, blond young woman struck up a friendship with Ferrell, but it would be six years before anything more than a friendly relationship would develop.

Looking for the Light

Ferrell continued to try his luck at stand-up comedy, but could not seem to get the hang of it. He was faced with the dilemma of trying to find a venue in which he could exhibit his comic talent without the pressure of having to be funny on demand. The answer would come in a most unlikely forum, and in fact Ferrell would not realize it at the time.

While still in college he had been pulled up onstage to join in during a skit by the Los Angeles improvisational group the

Ferrell shows his goofy side at a New York Knicks game. Soon after college, Ferrell decided to pursue a career in show business as a comedian.

Groundlings. He readily admits to not being very good, but he loved the freedom and camaraderie that improv comedy allowed him. He explains:

> I didn't realize it at the time, but I was actually suppressing those types of performance urges. It didn't go off like a light bulb, like, "I'm going to go into comedy! I'm going to do this." . . . It wasn't until later that I thought, "There's still nothing that seems to quite interest me the way that did, so I'm going to take a shot at improv and try some standup, if I can get up the nerve." So it kind of slowly developed.[17]

Having finally gotten up the nerve to attempt something he had both avoided and searched for, Ferrell began to seriously consider pursuing a show business career. He hesitated, however, remembering the instability that had plagued his father's career as a musician.

Helping him make the decision to abandon the unfulfilling world of day jobs was a short stint as a teller for Wells Fargo Bank. Ferrell consistently came up short at the end of his shifts, earning many lectures from his manager, which left him more despondent than ever. "I was miserable," he says of that time. "I remember telling my mom I would rather do standup naked on *The Tonight Show* than work in a bank."[18]

Joining the Team

Knowing he could no longer continue along the path he was on, but still dreading the idea of having to be funny standing alone against the glare of a comedy stage spotlight, Ferrell decided to look into the improv comedy he had tried while at USC. Just as he had excelled at team sports in high school, he felt he might have a better chance to excel at being funny as a member of a team than as a solo performer.

In 1991 Ferrell decided to move out of his mother's home and back to Los Angeles. He sought out The Groundlings Theater on Melrose Avenue and inquired about improv classes. The four-part curriculum at the Groundlings school consists of basic, intermediate, lab, and advanced classes in a systematic approach

Ferrell poses with Cheri Oteri, a woman he met in Los Angeles when he joined an improvisational group known as the Groundlings.

to both writing and performing improvisational sketch comedy. Some graduates of the advanced class are elected by other members to join the Sunday Company, where they are nurtured to become regular Groundlings cast members.

When the twenty-four-year-old Ferrell enrolled in the classes, he joined other novice actors such as Chris Kattan, Ana Gasteyer, and Cheri Oteri. They, along with several dozen others, learned how to turn a simple premise or character into a full-fledged performance piece.

It was an environment in which Ferrell felt perfectly at home. He did not have to be funny all the time—he only had to create situations and characters from which the comedy would come forth organically. "At the Groundlings it wasn't necessarily about saying funny things or writing funny lines, because I could never really do that unless they came out of improvisation or the situation," Ferrell remembers. "My strengths were always playing a certain attitude or level of commitment, or just playing it straight while juxtaposed with whatever stupid situation I found myself in."[19]

Making Ends Meet

The four-part curriculum of the school and the camaraderie of ensemble performing were very much to Ferrell's liking. He excelled at everything that was required of him and moved up the ranks of the performers. By 1992 he had become a full-fledged cast member and began creating some of the characters he would later make famous on *Saturday Night Live.* At the same time, he began to audition for other acting roles.

Since the pay at the Groundlings was meager, Ferrell still had to find odd jobs to make ends meet. Viveca Paulin, his friend from Costa Mesa College, worked at the prestigious auction house Butterfield & Butterfield and helped Ferrell get a job as an appraisal coordinator, organizing estates to be appraised by the firm's experts, who would then accept or decline the items for auction. The job fit Ferrell's needs: It was close to where he lived and offered a fairly flexible schedule that allowed him to go out on auditions.

He would sometimes go home for lunch to watch whatever baseball game he had been listening to on the radio. When the Chicago Cubs played, Ferrell loved listening to the late Cubs' announcer Harry Caray. He found Caray's speech pattern so amusing, he began doing a dead-on impression that he worked into sketches with the Groundlings.

In spite of his day job's flexible schedule, auditioning for acting roles and working for the auction house quickly came into conflict with each other. Ferrell dealt with the conflict by sticking by a personal rule. "I made a rule for myself that it was just a job to subsist and that if I started getting auditions based on my work with the Groundlings, even at the expense of getting fired, I would go,"[20] he says.

When he had an audition, Ferrell tried to schedule his lunch hour accordingly. One audition found him waiting more than four hours to try out for a commercial. When he nervously returned to the office, he discovered that no one had noticed he was gone. From then on he became very casual about his job. When his boss confronted him about his absences, Ferrell not only owned up to the misconduct, he also volunteered that he was not doing very well. His boss was so taken aback by this forthrightness that he simply agreed with Ferrell's assessment of his job performance and left him alone.

Gaining Momentum

Luckily for Ferrell, his acting career was gaining momentum, so such confrontations no longer concerned him. He and fellow Groundlings cast member Chris Kattan had developed the now-popular grunting characters the Butabi brothers, disco regulars who obnoxiously attempted to dance with any female patron who crosses their path. It was not their bizarre gyrations that drew laughter, but the fact that no matter how many times they were rejected, they continued their behavior unabated. This proved to be an early example of Ferrell's ability to garner laughs through acts of outrageous hubris.

Ferrell and Kattan also found work during the holidays as Santa Claus and one of his helpers. Ferrell remembers, "Kattan was my elf at this outdoor mall in Pasadena for five weeks, passing out candy canes. It was hilarious because little kids could care less about the elf. They just come right to Santa Claus. So by the second weekend, Kattan had dropped the whole affectation he was doing and was like (Ferrell makes a face of bitter boredom), 'Santa's over there, kid.'"[21]

Ferrell was able to find other work, but not just to make ends meet. His auditions were resulting in paid work appearing on such TV shows as the sitcoms *Grace Under Fire* and *Living Single*, and the cable comedy show *Strangers with Candy*. He was also featured in the black comedy *Bucket of Blood*, a made-for-cable TV movie.

In 1998 Chris Kattan and Will Ferrell arrive in character for the New York premiere of A Night at the Roxbury. *Kattan was also a member of the Groundlings.*

It seemed just a matter of time before his momentum would result in even more impressive work.

Chance of a Lifetime

By May 1995 Ferrell had fully honed his ability to bring characters and premises to life before the eyes of appreciative Groundlings audiences. His natural likeability and upbeat spirit brought to life humorous and believable characters often made even funnier based on the situations they were put in.

When he had been with the Groundlings main company for about six months, Ferrell was one of several cast members noticed by Marci Klein, a producer of *Saturday Night Live* (SNL). On the lookout for new talent for the show's upcoming season, Klein approached Ferrell about coming to New York to audition for the show's executive producer and cocreator Lorne Michaels.

At the audition, Ferrell performed what he considered some of his best and most polished material, including such conceptual impressions as Harry Caray auditioning for a play, Ted Kennedy doing stand-up comedy, and a seemingly normal busi-

In 1995 Ferrell auditioned for producer Lorne Michaels in hopes of joining the cast of Saturday Night Live.

Will Ferrell on the Difference Between Second City and the Groundlings

When *Playboy* magazine reporter David Resnin sat down with Will Ferrell in 2001, he asked him about the difference between Second City and the Groundlings. Ferrell replied, "In broad strokes, Groundlings is more wacky, more character driven. Second City is more theater with a point. The Groundlings rarely did a sketch that commented on Los Angeles or politics. Social commentary seems to run through all of Second City's shows. Some view Second City as smarter, Groundlings as dumber."

ness executive who likes to play with cat toys. One piece showed impressive skill and timing on Ferrell's part. He perfectly created the aura of a weekend backyard barbecue as a proud middle-class dad showing off his grilling skills for the neighbors. A casual comment to his rambunctious offspring playing nearby slowly escalated into a full-blown verbal attack on his own children. Ferrell's growing intensity during an otherwise leisurely paced scene showed off his impeccable timing as well as the ability to create a dramatically comic moment out of thin air. He passed the audition.

The Briefcase

The next phase of the SNL audition was a meeting with Michaels and several of the show's other producers. Anticipating disaster if he was perceived as anything but hilarious, Ferrell devised a plan to keep the humor flowing during the meeting. He brought with him a briefcase full of fake money and planned to keep piling it all on the desk as Michaels spoke.

When the meeting began, Ferrell noticed immediately that the atmosphere, at least for him, was far too tense to carry out his gag. He held the briefcase tightly as Michaels explained to him how the show would work if he became a cast member. The moment to utilize the contents of the briefcase never presented itself, but Ferrell nevertheless brought the prop along every time he had to meet with Michaels.

After several more meetings with Michaels, Ferrell took note of something other than the best time to open his briefcase: He had yet to hear whether he was actually hired for the show or not. With each successive meeting, it seemed to Ferrell that Michaels was just trying to get to know him better. Ferrell says,

> The way he told me was, "So, we'll bring you out to New York," and I thought, "Oh, another audition." Then he said, "Have you ever lived in New York?" And that's when it hit me: Oh, I got the job. Then I felt self-conscious because I was so relaxed and I wasn't jumping up and down, and so I was like, "Oh, okay." And then I said to Lorne, "Well, I'm going to shake your hand." And he was like, "Do whatever you need to do." And then I walked out.[22]

To this day, the briefcase full of fake money remains in Ferrell's possession.

Chapter 3

The Best Utility Man in Comedy

Frrom its first broadcast in 1975, SNL has proven to be one of the most controversial shows in TV history. Over the years, the show has changed casts, producers, and writers many times. By the early 1990s, recasting and retooling resurrected its sagging popularity, but executives at NBC found the current crew of mostly young stand-up comics obnoxious and unfunny. Michaels was forced to fire almost everyone in the cast as he and his associates set out again to bring SNL back to its former glory—hoping it was not too late. Michaels and company knew one of the most important ingredients to succeeding with a new cast would be a dependable utility man, capable of doing whatever was asked of him while being both funny and believable. They would soon discover that they had hired the best utility man in comedy.

The Pressure of Live TV

As a fledgling cast member of SNL, Ferrell was thrust into one of the most high-pressure situations in contemporary TV. The need to be funny as soon as possible was tangible to everyone in the cast. This was made obvious to the new cast members by virtue of the fact that they were on the show strictly on a prove-yourself basis. Ferrell's contract was initially for only nine shows, which could be extended to six more if his bosses liked what they saw. After that, he would have to wait to find out if he was being brought back for the next year. "And then after that it was year by year, and so you always feel like you're a little bit on shaky ground,"[23] recalls Ferrell.

Along with anxiety over whether they would be employed the following year, Ferrell and the cast had to live with an intense work schedule. Every Tuesday the cast spent twenty-four hours coming up with and perfecting sketches that might be used on the extremely collaborative show. Wednesday was the read-through, in which cast and writers exchanged ideas to be used or discarded, depending mostly on Michaels's decision. Cast and writers would continue to polish sketches up to and after Friday night's dress rehearsal before a live audience. It was not unusual for Michaels to cut sketches just before airtime—or even in the middle of the live show, which was broadcast to millions of viewers on Saturday night.

"Get Off the Shed!"

From the very first time the 1995 cast got together at their first Tuesday brainstorming session, Ferrell felt the immense pressure to succeed. One of the first things the writers asked of Ferrell was to perform a character he had done for his audition. It was one thing to do a character like the backyard dad who screams unmercifully at his children for an audition; to use this not-very-sympathetic personage in Ferrell's debut performance on SNL was something else altogether.

On Saturday, September 30, 1995, Ferrell appeared on the opening show of *Saturday Night Live*'s twenty-first season. As planned, his first major sketch was the backyard barbecue entitled "Get Off the Shed!"—the unheeded command Ferrell shouts to his off-camera children. As the sketch progressed and the intensity of Ferrell's performance grew, the studio audience and those watching at home laughed uproariously. Playing the maniacally abusive father, as well as several other characters throughout the night, made Ferrell an immediate standout in the new cast. Whether he was capable of being the show's utility actor remained an open question. To some, such as Ken Tucker, a TV critic for *Entertainment Weekly*, that possibility seemed highly unlikely: "Most annoying newcomer: Will Ferrell, whose yelled-insult shtick became intolerably annoying halfway through the debut."[24]

Ferrell poses at his New York apartment in a smoking jacket and hunting boots. Ferrell's ability to play a wide variety of characters made him a favorite SNL cast member.

For Ferrell, the toughest hurdle was surviving his first week on the show. Several years later he told an interviewer, "There was a part of me that could have quit after the very first time I was on the show. Really. It was like, 'Wow, I did it. I was on an episode of Saturday Night Live,' and I almost wanted to keep it pristine."[25] He had no time to breathe a sigh of relief, however, as the pace of the show required him to do the same thing all over again the following week, starting with a new brainstorming session on Tuesday.

The Spartan Cheerleaders

Ferrell's next hurdle was to confront him again and again. Since the show was collaborative, he and the rest of the tight-knit cast had to help create and execute sketches each week. Some characters and situations were recurring, but completely new material was needed each week as well. Aiding him considerably was the versatility of fellow cast members such as Molly Shannon and Darrell Hammond, and former Groundlings Chris Kattan, Ana Gasteyer, and Cheri Oteri.

One of Ferrell's most memorable characters was created over the summer before his first season on the show. He and Oteri were walking around the stage area to get a feel for the space they would be working in, which was Studio 8H in New York's Rockefeller Center. The acoustics were such that Oteri began stamping her feet rhythmically for effect, and, in short order, Ferrell joined in with handclaps. The two actors began to play with different ideas, and before long they had created two overly enthusiastic high school cheerleaders. "We stumbled across the fact that she'd been a cheerleader in high school, and I used to love watching the ESPN cheerleading championships,"[26] recalls Ferrell.

A month after Ferrell's debut on the show, he and Oteri first performed as Spartan cheerleaders Craig and Ariana. Over the next two years they would re-create these characters, among the most memorable in the history of the show, almost twenty times. When such guest stars as Jim Carrey and Pamela Anderson hosted the show, they specifically asked to be in a cheerleaders sketch with Ferrell and Oteri.

The Best Utility Man in Comedy   41

Not everyone who watched the show found the cheerleaders amusing, however, as Ferrell discovered when he logged onto an Internet chat room to see what some TV viewers thought of the show. "The first comment that came was, 'That guy Will Ferrell, he's really funny.' I thought, oh, this isn't so bad," recalls Ferrell. "The very next comment was, '. . . We should take him out and drag him behind a car.' That taught me not to go sniffing around too much."[27]

"Live from New York, it's Saturday night!"

Those words were first spoken to open the irreverent comedy show on October 11, 1975, and have been used to open every show since. The original cast, the Not Ready For Prime Time Players, consisted of Dan Aykroyd, John Belushi, Chevy Chase, Jane Curtin, Garrett Morris, Laraine Newman, and Gilda Radner. The show was originally called *NBC's Saturday Night*; cocreator Lorne Michaels was allowed to call it *Saturday Night Live* in 1976, upon cancellation of a variety show of the same name on a rival network. Many of the cast were also writers on the show, improv veterans who created dozens of skits and characters that have become icons of popular culture.

After five years and many accolades, the original cast left the show and Michaels quit as the show's executive producer. Some of the key cast members found success in Hollywood, but unfortunately, John Belushi died of a drug overdose in 1980, and Gilda Radner died of cancer in 1989. Back at SNL, a new cast seemed to pop up every couple of seasons, with varying degrees of success. Michaels returned to the show and has been executive producer since 1985.

Some features of SNL have remained constant for nearly three decades: Every ninety-minute show starts with what is called a cold opening, a sketch that has no introduction. The sketch ends with someone onstage shouting, "Live from New York, it's Saturday night!" After the opening credits, the celebrity guest host does a monologue, and several skits then follow a commercial parody. A fake news segment called "Weekend Update," in which current events are spoofed, follows a musical guest performance. There are then a few more skits and, if time allows, the musical guest has an encore. At 12:58 A.M. Eastern Standard Time, the cast, musical guest, and any cameo performers join the host onstage to say good night. Michaels and his comedy alchemists manage to do this twenty times a year, with reruns in between to give everyone a short respite.

Fellow SNL actor Mike Myers (right) gave Ferrell his first movie role in the 1997 blockbuster Austin Powers: International Man of Mystery.

Doing It All

Ferrell managed to incorporate some of the work he had performed at the Groundlings into his work on *Saturday Night Live.* He and Kattan recreated their head-bobbing disco lounge losers the Butabi brothers for a much wider audience. Ferrell also performed his Harry Caray impression, which had originated at the Groundlings and was later part of his SNL audition.

Ferrell survived to his second season of SNL and continued to tackle whatever was asked of him. When federal authorities captured the infamous Unabomber, Ted Kaczynski, SNL writers devised the idea of portraying the psychotic hermit as a free-wheeling party animal without a care in the world. Ferrell played the role to the hilt.

He found himself playing supporting characters in other performers' recurring sketches, and his performances not only added to the scene, but sometimes stole the show. When SNL made fun of the celebrities who appear on the game show *Jeopardy*, others in the cast did dead-on impressions of the stars. Ferrell played host Alex Trebek as if every ridiculous comment uttered by the celebrities brought him to the brink of his own sanity. His ability to make even the most outrageous concept believable and still get laughs was proof that SNL had its new utility player. "Molly Shannon and I used to talk about this on SNL," Ferrell says, "about how we approached all the sketches as little acting pieces. Even with the most outlandish character, it works to approach it as if what I'm doing here is the real thing."[28]

After two full seasons of making the outlandish believable on SNL, Ferrell was gaining recognition. The show's ratings were rising, and catchphrases of popular characters were once again being repeated across the country. With an impressive backlog of successes at tackling any character assigned to him, Ferrell began branching into other areas of pop culture. He made his debut on the big screen with a small role in the wildly successful 1997 comedy *Austin Powers: International Man of Mystery*. The film was a vehicle for former SNL cast member Mike Myers, who played the dual role of swinging '60s spy Austin Powers and his nemesis, Dr. Evil. Myers later said that in developing the character Dr. Evil, he had based his strange voice pattern on SNL producer Michaels's voice. Ferrell's character, Dr. Evil's henchman Mustafa, is disposed of early in the film.

A Night at the Roxbury

One of Ferrell's projects during this period offered a larger role than his brief appearance in the first Austin Powers film. He and Chris Kattan were approached to make a film version of the popular disco characters the Butabi brothers. Michaels and director Amy Heckerling wanted to produce a film called *A Night at the*

Roxbury, in which the sketch characters would be fleshed out. Ferrell, Kattan, and SNL writer Steve Koren wrote a screenplay in which the brothers worked in their father's florist shop and desperately tried to open their own nightclub while still living at home.

Playing a lead role in the film, Ferrell was able to get a small role for his brother, Patrick, as well as Viveca Paulin, whom he was now dating. Ferrell expressed concern about the project

Ferrell and Chris Kattan reprised their SNL roles as the disco-dancing Butabi brothers in the 1998 film A Night at the Roxbury.

when the film was in production, saying, "The worst thing is, these characters really hadn't talked, so it was a blank page when we started. Either people are going to love it or they'll say, 'Why don't they shut up?'"[29]

When the film came out in October 1998, its fate was similar to that of several other films based on SNL characters: Audiences stayed away and critics deemed it unwatchable, an eight-minute sketch painfully stretched into a two-hour movie. Many fans have approached Ferrell over the years and boasted of having seen the film many times; Ferrell's only reaction is to apologize profusely.

In one of the few memorable sequences in the film, Ferrell and Kattan are shown strolling the beach wearing nothing but thongs. Such outrageous behavior would soon become a hallmark of Ferrell's work.

More Memorable Characters

Other roles followed for Ferrell, who worked diligently on film projects when SNL was finished for the season. The year 1999 saw the release of three films in which Ferrell appeared. He played journalist Bob Woodward in *Dick*, a parody of the Watergate saga; he was Sky Corrigan, the love interest to Molly Shannon's SNL character Mary Katherine Gallagher in the film *Superstar*; and he reprised the role of Mustafa in *Austin Powers: The Spy Who Shagged Me*. Only the last film fared well at the box office.

Back at SNL, Ferrell continued to create memorable characters with his quirky brand of humor. His talent expanded in playing characters who were walking examples of hubris—people who were not nearly as smart as they thought they were or who were incredibly enthusiastic in the face of rejection. In one popular sketch, Ferrell and Gasteyer performed as music teachers struggling to be hip as they sing popular tunes to their unappreciative student audience. He also played a very creepy version of James Lipton, the popular host of the cable TV show *Inside the Actor's Studio*, who gushes over his celebrity guests.

One of Ferrell's most talked-about incarnations was his impression of Attorney General Janet Reno. This idea came from

Will Ferrell's Opinion of SNL's Worst Host

Authors Tom Shales and James Andrew Miller interviewed Ferrell for *Live from New York*, their book about SNL. When they asked him who he thought the worst guest host ever was, he gave a surprisingly detailed response:

> The worst host was Chevy Chase. He was here the first year we were here and then came back the next year and that was the kicker, the following year. It started right from the Monday pitch; you could just tell something was up. I don't know if he was on something or what, if he took too many back pills that day or something, but he was just kind of going around the room and systematically riffing. First it was on the guys, playfully making fun until, when he got to one of the female writers, he made some reference. . . . I've never seen Lorne more embarrassed and red.
>
> In hindsight, I wish we'd all gotten up and walked out of the room. It was just bad news. I will have to say that Chevy's been nothing but nice to me personally, and I think he thinks I'm funny, so I'm cool with him, but yeah, he's been quote-unquote the roughest host.

Paulin, who suggested that Ferrell play Reno, who, like him, is over six feet tall. The couple laughed at the idea of Ferrell playing Reno as a big, imposing woman who knocks things over and threatens people with violence when they visit her teen dance TV show.

The sketch proved so popular that one night Reno herself put on a blue dress like the one Ferrell wore and joined him onstage during the skit. "I was a little nervous about meeting her, but she had a great attitude about it," says Ferrell. "I told her that we've always portrayed her as a take-charge, almost superhero kind of character, and she kind of went, 'Oh, be quiet!'"[30]

Dealing with Success

Playing Janet Reno and other successful characters on SNL did not change Ferrell's basic lifestyle. Because success came to him gradually, he was able to maintain his equilibrium in the face of growing stardom. In spite of SNL's grueling schedule, he managed to fly back to Los Angeles every few weeks to be with his girlfriend. He still drove a 1984 Toyota Camry he had purchased many years before, and he still called Paulin whenever it broke down.

During the time Ferrell worked on SNL, he shared a modest five-hundred-square-foot Manhattan apartment with his brother, Patrick, an aspiring actor who worked as Ferrell's regular understudy. Ferrell's attitude was a direct result of his leisurely paced success. "I've been so lucky," he says. "It's all been relatively gradual. . . . But it works to your advantage. You just slowly get used to getting recognized here and there. I always feel like I'm the guy who snuck into a black-tie party wearing a loud Hawaiian shirt. No one's kicked me out yet, but I'm still waiting to get kicked out."[31]

Success and Failure

Ferrell's misgivings were to some extent realistic, since not all of his work on SNL was well received. Several of his ideas never made it on the air. When guest host Tom Hanks appeared on the show, Ferrell thought it would be funny to do a skit spoofing Hanks's film *Apollo 13*. The film retold the true story of the aborted moon landing in which astronauts had to fend for themselves when dealing with an in-flight mechanical malfunction. The phrase they used to alert mission control–"Houston, we have a problem"–has become part of the cultural lexicon as an understated way of referring to impending disaster. Ferrell thought the phrase could be used in a skit in which one astronaut confesses his love for another. Ferrell has suggested the skit was turned down because Hanks thought it would be inappropriate.

Such incidents were relatively rare, however, since for many viewers Ferrell's work was a reason to keep watching the show. SNL producer Michaels, who rarely comments publicly, acknowledged the importance of Ferrell's contribution: "Will is the glue that holds the show together. He's the first choice of the writers for almost every sketch. His style is not so strong that it overwhelms the writing."[32]

Others echoed Michaels's acknowledgment of Ferrell's value to the show. Longtime fans and critics of SNL felt he was a utility man in the tradition of former cast members Dan Aykroyd and Phil Hartman, which the show had been sorely missing. Ferrell's costar and close friend Kattan agreed with Michaels's assessment, adding some compliments of his own: "Will gets written for a lot because he's you know, an Everyman. He's hilarious, he's brilliant, and the writers love him more than anybody. I think Will is even better than Phil Hartman in some ways. He's the utility man, yes, but he also has characters like the Cheerleaders and the Roxbury guys that I do with him."[33]

Tying the Knot

When the year 2000 rolled around, it seemed that life could not possibly get any better for Ferrell. His popularity on SNL had grown, but not fast enough to overwhelm him. His film career may not have been highly successful, but as a good supporting comedy

In 2000 Ferrell married college friend and actress Viveca Paulin.

actor he could always find work in movies. He was capable of play-ing both leads and supporting roles in films. Greater success was only a matter of finding the right vehicle.

Life for Ferrell was taking off, and it seemed like the best time to ascend to the next step in his personal life as well. In 2000 he and Paulin got married. Ferrell jokingly says, "I knew when I met her: She's the one. I'm just gonna wait. I'm just gonna wait for her to come around the bend."[34]

It seemed all that Ferrell lacked was success in movies. That would eventually come to pass, but in the immediate future he would have even greater success with a new character he was asked to perform on SNL.

Chapter 4

Small Screen to Big Screen

FERRELL'S ABILITY TO excel at almost anything requested of him on SNL pointed the way to the next logical step: attempting similar success in movies. Previous SNL stars such as Bill Murray, Eddie Murphy, Adam Sandler, and Mike Myers had all achieved even greater fame in films. Most former SNL cast members, however, had enjoyed much more modest success. Ferrell knew the key was in finding the right project to showcase his talent for mining comedy gold. He knew the odds were against him, but he was determined to try.

Drowning Mona and The Ladies Man

The new century ushered in a new chance for film success for Ferrell. His first film of the millennium appeared in March 2000 and was not a promising omen. The film, called *Drowning Mona*, was a dark comedy in which several small-town residents are suspected of killing a very unpopular neighbor. Ferrell's contribution is a glorified cameo as a very strange funeral director named Cubby. With a part so small, Ferrell had as little to do with the film's failure as he did with the popularity of *Austin Powers*.

The failure of *Drowning Mona* did not keep Ferrell from working steadily in films. In October 1999 he filmed *The Ladies Man*, a feature-film version of another popular SNL sketch. In the sketch, veteran cast member Tim Meadows portrays Leon Phelps, a smooth-talking, chauvinistic radio host whose sole concern in life is dating as many women as possible. The film version begins with Phelps being fired from his job and then follows his attempts to regain his livelihood, his romantic conquests, and redeem his life while running from a vigilante group of men—the angry husbands and boyfriends of his conquests.

Ferrell costarred as Lance Delune, the leader of the vigilante group. The film's director, Reginald Hudlin, was very impressed by Ferrell: "I can't say enough about the pleasure of working with Will Ferrell. Will is the consummate comedian. . . . He is a fountain of creativity. He is constantly coming up with new jokes, new ideas, new takes."[35] Producer Bob Klein joined the chorus singing Ferrell's praises: "When it came time to cast the part of Lance, for me there was only Will Ferrell. . . . he can take any material and just raise it several levels. . . . He's great with the spaces between the lines. He takes a character and really owns it. . . . Stuff that wasn't necessarily designed to get laughs because of the strength of his character delivers more because it is Will Ferrell doing it."[36]

Ferrell is on record as having enjoyed working on the film, especially a song-and-dance number that comes toward the film's climax, in which his character gives a speech extolling the virtues of manliness—and then leads his cohorts in a very unmanly song. It proved to be a highlight in an otherwise disappointing film that went the way of most SNL features. Following its release in October 2000, critics wasted no time in comparing *The Ladies Man* to at least a dozen other failed attempts to transfer popular SNL sketches to the big screen.

Back at SNL

His lack of film success certainly did not slow down Ferrell's work schedule. In early 2001 he lent his voice to the lead character of an animated series called *The Oblongs*. Ferrell's character is the father of a family that lives near a chemical waste dump, and as a result, all of the Oblongs suffer from some form of toxic side effect. Part of the dark humor is derived from Ferrell's armless, legless character's sunny disposition. This type of humor had a hard time finding an audience on national television and consequently the series aired only seven episodes after its April 1, 2001, debut.

SNL still occupied the majority of Ferrell's time. While other projects came and went with little fanfare, Ferrell could still claim a high level of achievement on the popular late-night comedy. He was still helping to create new and varied characters while doing new sketches of his established characters. He added to his growing gallery an impression of pop singer Neil Diamond as well as Robert Goulet, whom Ferrell depicted as singing hip hop songs, which the once-popular baritone is not likely to have covered.

What these and other Ferrell incarnations have in common is an inflated sense of self-importance or pomposity that comes across

The cast of The Ladies Man, *another movie based on an SNL skit, pose at the Hollywood premiere in 2000. The film was a box-office flop.*

as funny. The most popular example of this is a character he created with new cast member Rachel Dratch. Dratch had told Ferrell that when she was in college she had a female professor who seemed to take everything too seriously and boasted about her love life.

At Ferrell's urging, the two actors set about creating a sketch. They played a couple who called each other "luh-vuh" and bragged incessantly about their romantic accomplishments to anyone in their presence. The sketch always ended with Ferrell dropping his affectation and shouting about his bad back. "The first time at read-through we could not get through it, just like on the show we cannot get through it," recalls Dratch. "I try not to laugh too much, because I don't like it when I'm watching TV and I see someone breaking up all the time; it becomes sort of cheap. But sometimes you just can't help it. . . . Will will just make a face or something and it just gets me."[37]

The Presidential Election

The popularity of the "luh-vuhs" paled in comparison to Ferrell's next major assignment, which garnered Ferrell more attention than anything else he had done before and put his talent at the forefront of the cultural landscape. Ultimately, it also proved to be the biggest obstacle in furthering his career beyond SNL: His portrayal of one character was so impressive that for a while it seemed that was all anyone wanted to see him do.

SNL's humor had moved away from political commentary over the years, but as the 2000 presidential election heated up, the writers could not ignore the humor that could be evoked by the two major parties' candidates. Resident impressionist Darrell Hammond was the first cast member to attempt a parody of Republican candidate George W. Bush, but for all of his efforts, Hammond seemed better suited to play Democratic candidate Al Gore.

Ferrell assumed the role of Bush in late 1999 at Michaels's request and continued to play the Texas governor as just another of his wildly funny characters. As the campaign intensified, Ferrell portrayed Bush more often in mock debates and press conferences on the show. By exaggerating certain characteristics—

Modern Presidential Humor

The huge popularity of Will Ferrell's impression of President George W. Bush prompted a revival in presidential humor. In 2003 *Newsweek* gave its readers a quick rundown of some previous highlights of such humor since the early 1960s:

1963: JFK impersonator Vaughn Meader wins the Grammy for album of the year for "The First Family," his spoof of the Kennedy clan.

1967: Pete Seeger appears on "The Smothers Brothers Comedy Hour" to sing about "the big fool" Lyndon Johnson.

1968: Richard Nixon appears on NBC's naughty "Rowan & Martin's Laugh-In" and delivers their signature line, "Sock it to me."

1973: Gov. Ronald Reagan is the first guest roasted on "The Dean Martin Show."

1976: President Ford, satirized repeatedly on "Saturday Night Live" as a klutz, appears on the show and tells Chevy Chase: "I'm Gerald Ford and you're not."

1988: After a boring speech at the Democratic National Convention, Gov. Bill Clinton goes on "The Tonight Show" to joke about himself.

1990: Dana Carvey's wimpy, nasal characterization of President George H. W. Bush turns "wouldn't be prudent" into a national catchphrase. Bush later invites Carvey to the White House.

1992: Clinton, the Democratic presidential front runner, takes his sunglasses and his saxophone to "Arsenio Hall."

1992: After Vice President Quayle complains that "Murphy Brown" glorifies out-of-wedlock children, he becomes the butt of numerous jokes at the Emmy Awards.

1996: Bob Dole makes the rounds of late-night shows after losing the election.

2000: Gov. Bush appears on "Late Show" via satellite. Letterman: "How do you look so youthful and rested?" Bush: "Fake it." Letterman: "And that's pretty much how you're going to run the country?"

2000: "SNL's" Will Ferrell mocks Bush's mangled diction with one word: "strategery." During sketches on the debates, Darrell Hammond's stiff take on Gore is so convincing, the candidate's handlers make him study the show.

2000: "Daily Show" correspondent Steve Carell goes on John McCain's campaign bus and confounds the candidate with silly questions. McCain later plays the tape constantly for visitors.

2001: Comedy Central debuts "That's My Bush," the first sitcom about a president, from the creators of "South Park." It lasts all of eight episodes.

2003: John Kerry rides a motorcycle onto the set of "The Tonight Show," to the tune of "Easy Rider."

Ferrell spoofs President George W. Bush during a 2004 benefit show. Ferrell became famous for his uncanny ability to impersonate the president.

hesitant sentence structure and awkward facial gestures—Ferrell became nationally recognized as the best impressionist of the Republican candidate. He would smile at the wrong time during a speech, squint his eyes as if trying to think of something intelligent, but then finally respond with monosyllabic answers. "I go more for the physicality," Ferrell explains. "Maybe it's laziness, lack of skill or patience, but I think it only really takes one tic. Focus on that one thing and the rest falls into place."[38]

Ferrell played Bush much as he played his other characters: as someone not nearly as smart as he thought, constantly putting his foot in his mouth in the most embarrassing ways. Ferrell was named one of the fifty most important political figures in America by *George* magazine, and according to *Newsweek*, the campaigns of both parties watched the sketches for hints on how to win the popular vote.

The Curse of TV Success

When the election made daily front-page news following the debacle of the Florida recount and the Supreme Court decision that granted Bush the presidency, SNL's ratings reached their highest level in more than six years. America was tuning in each week to see Ferrell do his squinty-eyed version of the newly elected president's reaction to the week's events. Ferrell played Bush thirty times, more than any other character over the seven years he was on the show. Despite the attention, Ferrell publicly acknowledged his dislike of the new president. "People were like, 'Hey, you've got a job for four more years,' and I was like, 'Well, if I want to stay that long,'"[39] he says.

Making the transition from TV to film became even harder as Ferrell began to contemplate leaving the show. Unfortunately, his films had not generated much interest at the box office, while his work on SNL had created a huge following. He was nominated for an Emmy Award in 2001 in the category of Outstanding Individual Performance in a Variety or Music Program; he was one of the few cast members to ever be so honored in the show's twenty-six-year history. The producers, no longer worried about whether Ferrell would work out well on the show, renegotiated his contract. At $350,000 a year, he was now one of the show's highest-paid stars ever. Ferrell appreciated the praise but longed for a career like those of other successful SNL alumni. What he really desired was feature film success, as he said when Bill Murray hosted the show. "I wanted him to think I was funny," he says. "It was real tricky. I wanted to grab his leg and say, 'Take me with you.'"[40]

Zoolander

Success in feature films continued to elude Ferrell, who continued to strive for it. His next film, *Zoolander*, was based on a series of sketches poking fun at the pomposity of the fashion industry, created for cable TV by actor/comedian Ben Stiller. Stiller played Derek Zoolander, a clueless male model who becomes a pawn in an international effort to end restrictions on child labor laws. The mastermind behind the plan is the outrageous designer Jacobin Mugatu, played by Ferrell.

Ferrell appeared throughout the film dressed in outlandish costumes, hair designs, and attitudes in a parody of contemporary fashion designers, but he played the character in keeping with many of his earlier roles. The incredibly self-absorbed Mugatu is revealed to be New Jersey necktie salesman Jacob Moogberg. Ferrell attempted to understand the psyche of his character by observing the way many actual designers behaved. "I watched footage of like, Jean Paul Gaultier and Alexander McQueen," he says, "and I got a little taste of how it's almost more about these guys than their clothes, I mean, McQueen rode out on a skateboard at the end of his show."[41]

But Ferrell's work in researching his part and his outrageous performance as Mugatu could not salvage the film. Like the unsuccessful SNL films, as funny as it may have appeared as a short sketch, *Zoolander* did not click with audiences as a feature film. Perhaps the audiences were unable to sympathize with any of the characters over the course of two hours, or perhaps Stiller, Ferrell, and the rest of the cast were too well known in other roles to be believable in their parts. Whatever the reason, the paradox of SNL success contrasted against the failure of his films was a puzzle Ferrell could not unravel. When asked about it, he simply says, "That's a good question that I don't have an answer for. I don't really know. All you have in comedy in general is to go with your instincts. You can only hope that other people think what you think is funny."[42]

Kevin Smith's World

Following *Zoolander* Ferrell had a small role in the 2001 film *Jay and Silent Bob Strike Back*. Created by cult director Kevin Smith, who played Silent Bob alongside Jason Mewes's Jay, the story follows the misadventures of two lead characters, first seen in minor roles in Smith's 1994 film *Clerks*. Smith constructed the film as a

Director Kevin Smith gave Ferrell a small part as Marshal Willenholly in the 2001 film Jay and Silent Bob Strike Back.

response to critics who had turned up their noses at *Clerks* and such follow-up films as 1995's *Mallrats* and 1997's *Chasing Amy.* In *Jay and Silent Bob* Smith chose to have his characters travel cross-country, encountering many adventures and characters along the way, including many from Smith's previous films.

One character who has an ongoing feud with the title heroes is the frantically misguided federal wildlife Marshal Willenholly, played by Ferrell. The name was derived from Marshall, Will, and Holly, who were the lead characters on the popular 1970s children show *Land of the Lost*. Such inside references are rampant in the film, which boasted many guest stars and in-jokes that Smith's loyal fan base reveled in. The rest of the filmgoing audience that saw the film when it was released in August 2001 were left scratching their heads in befuddlement.

September 11, 2001

Ferrell was back in New York for the next season of SNL by the time *Jay and Silent Bob* hit theaters. Neither he nor anyone else on the show had any inkling what was to occur just prior to the show's season debut. In the morning hours of September 11, two passenger jet airliners were crashed by terrorists into the towers of the World Trade Center; moments later, a third plane was crashed into the Pentagon in Washington, D.C.; and a fourth was crashed into a field in Pennsylvania. Thousands of people died in what was the worst attack on civilians in U.S. history.

The grief the nation felt was overwhelming, making the live comedy show seem almost irrelevant. At the offices of SNL, preparations for the September 29 debut episode were being reconsidered. Once the decision was made to go ahead with the show, producer Marci Klein had a difficult time getting the scheduled guest host to appear. She recalls a conversation concerning just that issue with the agent for the star who was trying to bow out; Klein told the agent, "On the grand scale of things, I just saw three thousand people die out my kitchen window. That's what matters."[43]

For Ferrell, still the most popular member of the cast, his emotions concerning the show after the attacks remained enigmatic. He says:

> I have a hard time figuring out what the viewpoint of the 9/11 show was. I guess in the final analysis you can't critique it the way you would any other show. The biggest

thing I'll take away from it was after the show—talking to firemen and policemen. They just kept thanking us and saying, "Thanks for the break, we really needed it," and we were going, "What? We should be thanking you."[44]

Ferrell was one of many big-name stars to appear in the Concert for New York City, held October 20 at Madison Square Garden. The show was broadcast live on HBO, and the audience in the arena consisted solely of the police, fire, and rescue workers who risked their lives during the tragedy. Ferrell appeared as President Bush and rallied the audience with his plans for abolishing the Taliban, the military rulers of Afghanistan, which had been the base of the 9/11 terrorists.

Making *Old School*

As the nation slowly recovered from the devastation, Ferrell began to reconsider leaving SNL. He was hard at work on his next project, a comedy entitled *Old School* that filmed in January 2002,

Meeting the President

It was inevitable that Will Ferrell would eventually meet his alter ego, President George W. Bush. Ferrell told *Playboy* his impression of the experience: "First, that he seemed ill at ease. Second, that he's tall as me. The last was of my being shoved out of the way so that someone at NBC could introduce him to Lorne Michaels' children. It was an awkward day. They said he really wanted to meet me, but I could tell that wasn't the case."

On the opposite end was what the president thought of meeting his alter ego. *U.S. News & World Report* printed this brief piece about the event in 2001:

Will Ferrell, Saturday Night Live's George W. Bush impersonator, thinks his subject is a dope, but that hasn't stopped the president-elect from making a kind offer: "I'd love to have him over to the White House," Bush tells our Kenneth T. Walsh. "Seriously, I would like for him to spend more personal time with me so he can get even better." Unlike his father, who loved to watch SNL's Dana Carvey say, "Wouldn't be prudent," Bush isn't a big fan and concedes that he didn't even know who Ferrell was when they met over the summer. But, he compliments, "I hear he's pretty darn good."

Vince Vaughn and Will Ferrell pose with the director of Old School, *a comedy about three friends who try to relive their wild college days.*

during SNL's holiday hiatus. On the set of the film he discussed the ramifications of leaving SNL: "I'm really trying to decide the best thing to do. There's an argument that maintaining a presence on the show means you have a nice platform in front of the public. At the same time, at some point you just have to take a flying leap. So . . . I don't know."[45]

He wrestled with what he would do for months while filming continued on *Old School.* Ferrell had become involved in the project after actor Vince Vaughn hosted SNL. The two struck up a friendship and agreed to work together on a suitable project. Actor Luke Wilson rounded out the trio of three established men who decide to relive their college days. As it turned out, Ferrell was the only one of the three actors who had actually finished college and participated in some of the characters' antics, such as streaking.

Wilson, who found Ferrell's intense style of acting almost too funny to work with, played the film's lead character. "He's got this total thousand-yard stare that's scary-hilarious," says Wilson. "There were times in a scene where I couldn't look at him—I'd look just off to the side of him—because otherwise I'd crack up."[46]

Making the Big Decision

Toward the end of filming *Old School*, Ferrell had made his decision. He informed the producers that he would be leaving, and it was agreed that his last regular appearance on SNL would be May 18, 2002. "I wanted to leave while I still thought of it fondly, as opposed to leaving after a year that was miserable," says Ferrell. "I was just ready to challenge myself with the next thing."[47]

Other big-name stars had left the show, but never with such a fanfare as Ferrell. The advance knowledge of his departure allowed ample time for the show's writers to cater to Ferrell more than ever before. He performed many of his best-known characters, such as *Jeopardy* host Alex Trebek and singer Neil Diamond—but this time he did so with the real Trebek and Diamond on stage with him.

After a career-making seven-year span of memorable performances, Ferrell said his good-bye at the end of the show, went to the bittersweet after-party, and returned to his wife in Los Angeles. Since *Old School* was not yet ready for release and his next scheduled film had not yet started filming, Ferrell spent the summer of 2002 unsure of what the future had in store for him.

Chapter 5

Breaking Through on Film

F ERRELL KNEW HE could not succeed in film until he broke free of the stigma of failed SNL spin-off films and characters audiences neither identified with nor found particularly sympathetic. Other SNL alumni, such as Chris Kattan, who starred in the ill-fated 2001 film *Corky Romano*, had faced the same dilemma. Having attempted film stardom in both lead and supporting roles, Ferrell knew his chances of success were dwindling rapidly. Only by finding the right vehicle to showcase his outrageousness and ability to display hubris in a comedic light could he achieve his goal.

Reaction to *Old School*

The vehicle Ferrell had been searching for was released on February 13, 2003. "Even though I miss the people [on SNL]," Ferrell told an interviewer, "*Old School* was the perfect thing to step into. I'm excited that this is coming out as the first thing after having been on the show—it's a nice thing to be a part of."[48]

Old School was an undeniable hit at the box office. Critics and audiences agreed that Ferrell's performance as Frank "the Tank" Ricard was the movie's highlight. He had finally found a character that audiences could both identify with and laugh hysterically at. Although the escapades of Frank are quite extreme, many audience members had known someone who, in spite of the best intentions, never really grew up.

At the start of the film, Ferrell's character is getting married and putting a wild past behind him. As he and his two friends indulge in their plan to resurrect their fraternity days, Frank's former self emerges. The most memorable scene has a drunken Frank removing all of his clothes and shouting that everyone was going streaking. He is halfway down an abandoned street before he realizes no one has joined him. Ferrell's character also demolishes a backyard children's party, referees a coed wrestling match, and helps kidnap a fraternity pledge from a grocery store parking lot.

The film eventually made more than $74 million at the box office. Its success manifested itself in strange ways for Ferrell. Not accustomed to such treatment, he found that admiring fans shouted lines from the film at him. "I have a bad memory for my own dialogue," he says. "Which makes it weird now because people will sometimes scream my lines at me on the street. . . . Sometimes I remember but sometimes I'm like, 'Oh, okay. Nice to meet you.'"[49]

Late-Night Talk Show Appearances

To help promote the film, Ferrell appeared on several talk shows, where another facet of his personality began to emerge. He was a frequent guest on *The Late Late Show with Craig Kilborn* and *Late Night with Conan O'Brien*, often showing up as Robert Goulet or another of the personalities he had created or imitated on SNL. On other occasions he would wear a shockingly brief outfit, such as a thong, and then act outrageously toward the host. Such behavior became the most talked-about aspect of Ferrell's talk show appearances, and he quickly gained an even greater reputation from it.

His ability to act so outrageously—including the famous streaking scene in *Old School*—harked back to Ferrell's high school days. Being known as a comedic actor, Ferrell understood the need to be funny in public, but his offstage persona is not naturally outrageous. As he had done when he was a place kicker for his high school football team, he blocked out his own personality and focused completely on the task at hand.

As a result, Ferrell easily donned the actor's cloak, so thoroughly inhabiting each role that the bizarre actions and outlandish personalities he displayed seemed to be coming directly from the characters. This talent for hiding his natural shyness behind the mask of a character began to emerge as early as high school and was polished during his stint at Costa Mesa College and the Groundlings, to compensate for Ferrell's inability to be funny on demand. "I'm just kind of not in that Robin Williams kind of mode or can easily access these things right away," he says. "I have to kind of think about it. And then people are like, 'Oh, yeah right. We've been waiting all day.' And then they're let down and disappointed, but what can I do?"[50]

Making a Christmas Classic

The raunchy R-rated humor of *Old School* finally afforded Ferrell a hit film, but his next project would be the extreme opposite. The

Ferrell performs a gymnastics routine in the highly successful comedy Old School, *his first film after leaving SNL.*

gentle, family-oriented humor of *Elf* was a radical departure from Ferrell's previous projects. Ferrell was signed to play the lead character, Buddy, who is raised as one of Santa's elves but in reality is a full-grown man with a child's personality. He leaves the North Pole to find his real father, a curmudgeonly book publisher to whom he teaches the true meaning of Christmas.

The script for *Elf* was written in 1996 but hung in limbo until the right actor could be found for the lead role. Bill Murray was first considered for the lead, but the box office success of *Old School* made studio executives take notice of Ferrell. Ferrell, in turn, was intrigued by the story. Actor/director Jon Favreau signed on for the project when he heard Ferrell would be playing Buddy. Screenwriter David Berenbaum was also glad to see Ferrell cast in the lead: "I think the movie just kind of waited for him to come along. I can't imagine anyone else in that role."[51]

From the very beginning of the project, everyone involved wanted *Elf* to be particularly special. "The key to a Christmas movie is the story and the message and the theme," explains Favreau. "On the one hand, I wanted to get big laughs and on the other hand, I wanted to make a movie that had the potential to be a classic that can be shown every year."[52]

The filmmakers set out to give the film a certain look, similar to that of a TV holiday special from the mid-1960s. The animation used in the North Pole scenes was reminiscent of the 1964 perennial TV classic *Rudolph the Red-Nosed Reindeer*. The sets and music were purposely created to seem familiar—as if they had been seen and heard before.

Forced Perspective

The most impressive technique the filmmakers used to accomplish their task was an old Hollywood trick not seen in recently made films. Ferrell had to appear much taller than the other actors in the scenes in which he is shown with fellow elves, and the producers decided to achieve this effect without using computers or any other new technology. Instead, they made the sets smaller for Ferrell, who was placed closer to the camera, and placed the other elf actors farther away from the

Will Ferrell, Marathon Man

Will Ferrell and his wife, Viveca, have become quite impressive marathon runners. In 2003 *Runner's World* magazine ran the following article by Amby Burfoot, entitled "Comedian Will Ferrell Hits the Roads: Live, from New York and Stockholm, It's Marathon Time." . . .

Will Ferrell and his wife, Viveca, ran the [2001] New York City Marathon in 5:01:56. "I'd always been an athlete and an occasional runner, and the marathon was just something I wanted to do," he says.

Afterward, nursing his post-race aches, Ferrell figured it was once and done. "Viveca was hooked, though," he says. "She wanted to run more marathons. And I began to wonder what I could do if I spent a full 26 weeks getting ready for the distance." Before New York City, his longest run had been barely 15 miles.

Soon Ferrell was working with Gary Kobat, a Los Angeles-based multisport athlete and personal coach who likes to say he's in the business of "personal transformation." His mantra: "To change your outcome, you've first got to change your thinking."

Under Kobat, Ferrell lost 25 pounds and saw his 10-K time drop from 53 minutes to 45. The next challenge: He decided to run the Stockholm Marathon in June. "Will could be the chapter in a textbook on doing things right," says Kobat. "He took his time, he built up gradually, he kept things simple, and he didn't overload the system."

The only part of the program that didn't cooperate was the Stockholm weather. It was 88 degrees at the start, and so blistering that the asphalt streets turned soft and sticky.

"Will was prepared to run close to 3:40," says Kobat, "but the heat forced us to totally change plans. It felt like Hawaii, not Stockholm, and Will's a big guy [6'3" and 195 pounds] who needs to stay hydrated to perform well."

Running together, Kobat, Will, and Viveca adjusted pace, and finished together in Stockholm's 1912 Olympic Stadium in 4:28:22. Ferrell didn't let the finish time disappoint him. He's had too much else to feel good about.

camera, making it appear as though the other actors were smaller than Ferrell.

This trick, known as forced perspective, works because the human eye sees things that are farther away as if they are smaller than an object that is closer. The execution, however, required

After his raunchy role in Old School, *Ferrell took on the part of Buddy, a grown man who believes he is an elf, in the 2003 Christmas movie,* Elf.

extreme attention to detail. Production designer Rusty Smith co-ordinated all aspects of the set without the use of modern technology. "Later on, when we tell people that there's no digital effects at all in the North Pole stuff," he says, "nobody will believe us because it looks so hyper real."[53]

Believing Buddy

Making the North Pole sequence work for an audience was only one of the movie's many objectives. The most important objective—making the audience care about what happens to the main character—was accomplished in large measure through Buddy's gentle, good-natured humor, derived mostly from the big elf's childlike enthusiasm in the face of modern cynicism. Favreau trusted Ferrell's instincts, and after the actor had done a scene as written, it might be reshot to allow Ferrell to improvise. When the script and production requirements allowed it, the version of a scene that was used in the finished film was usually Ferrell's improvisation.

For Ferrell, believing in Buddy was a major responsibility, but as far as he was concerned, the character's innate sweetness is what set the project apart from other holiday comedies. "I think in a lot of comedies there's a potential to not invest in the characters," he says. "With a character like Buddy you're interested in where the journey's going to take him."[54]

Much of the movie was filmed in Vancouver, British Columbia, and in New York City, with Ferrell deeply invested in the character throughout the filming. The sight of Ferrell in his brightly colored elf costume walking the streets of Manhattan drew very little reaction from world-weary New Yorkers. Ferrell, who totally embodied his character, would often spontaneously hug an unsuspecting passerby. "New Yorkers would just walk right past me and refuse to make eye contact. That would then provoke me to give them a hug," he explains. "People became really uncomfortable. Or they would yell 'Nice Tights!' The first day of filming was in the Lincoln Tunnel at seven in the morning. I didn't really get to warm up to the character. I just had to jump in."[55]

The Frat Pack

Filming completed on *Elf* in March 2003, and Ferrell began to line up his next projects. He returned to Los Angeles to be with his wife and their three dogs, a Labrador, a boxer, and a pointer. Even though Viveca was now successful in the auction business, and Ferrell's projects were growing rapidly, the couple decided to try and become parents.

Ferrell's agenda included filming a quick appearance in the film *Starsky & Hutch*, a comedy version of a popular 1970s TV cop show. Ferrell's *Zoolander* costars Ben Stiller and Owen Wilson played the title characters in the film, which derived most of its humor from making fun of '70s styles and fads. Tod Phillips, who had directed *Old School*, directed the film. Also making appearances in the film were *Old School* costars Vince Vaughn and Juliette Lewis. The only missing member of the gang was Owen Wilson's brother, Luke.

The frequent reteaming of many of the actors involved in these projects had piqued the interest of the media. Their most popular project resulted in the media dubbing them the "Frat Pack," but it was actually a result of just a good friendship formed out of a working relationship. Ferrell's growing popularity with filmgoers was a direct result of such media commentary. He felt the undue attention in celebrity-oriented periodicals rather silly and did not give it much weight. "It's not like there's a hot line—we're not calling each other saying, 'What are we gonna do next?'" Ferrell says. "It's that we're friends, like-minded people, and we think each other's funny."[56]

An Early Christmas Present

The media spotlight that Ferrell found himself increasingly immersed in was in no small part due to the prerelease chatter surrounding *Elf*. When the film opened in theaters on November 7, 2003, no one involved in the film could have anticipated the response.

The holiday season is extremely competitive for big-budget films, with studios releasing their most expensive films of the year in November and December to make the most money possible. The 2003 holiday season saw the release of the highly

New York City mayor Michael Bloomberg honors Will Ferrell, as he proclaims November 7, 2003, to be Elf Day.

anticipated computer-generated special effects sequel *Matrix: Revolutions* and the Russell Crowe swashbuckler *Master and Commander*. The film that made more money at the box office than either one of these films was the modestly budgeted *Elf*. It would go on to make more than $175 million and become one of the top-ten highest-grossing films of the year. The reaction Ferrell had to the news of *Elf*'s success was overwhelming: "How would I rate my happiness? Gleeful excitement—finished off with a slow wetting of my pants."[57]

Costars Christina Applegate and Ferrell appear in character to promote their 2004 movie, Anchorman: The Legend of Ron Burgundy.

Apparently, audiences shared the filmmakers' vision of *Elf* and wanted to believe in Buddy and hear the message of an old-fashioned holiday film. Several newspapers and magazines wrote commentaries on whether *Elf*'s success signalled a trend toward more family-oriented comedies. Ferrell himself was besieged with interviews asking him if he would be making more films for children, including an *Elf* sequel. He said only that he was not interested in focusing on one style of comedy and that he was hoping his next film would be a success.

First Girl in the Tree Fort

The reason for Ferrell's polite disclaimer was the vested interest he had in his next project. Former SNL writer Adam McKay and

Ferrell had collaborated on a screenplay that was as different as possible from *Elf*'s style of comedy. The idea came from a documentary Ferrell had seen while he was still on SNL. It detailed the life of a Southern California TV reporter in the early 1970s, who at one point coyly admitted to less-than-gentlemanly behavior when women entered his work environment. Both McKay and Ferrell found the man's story to be rife with comedy potential. Ferrell recalls, "He said, 'I have to be honest with you; I was a real male chauvinist pig,' and I said 'That's funny.'"[58]

Ferrell and McKay fashioned a screenplay for a comedy in which a female reporter invades the male-dominated world of local news in the 1970s, challenging the status quo. The film's working title, *First Girl in the Tree Fort*, summarized the plot. The collaborators held meetings with studio executives for several years but could not get anyone interested in their story, which was written in a style considered too bizarre to be successful.

After each failed attempt to sell their screenplay, McKay and Ferrell went back to the drawing board and did several rewrites. They changed a third-act ending in which all the main characters are involved in a mountainside plane crash, with cannibalism and bloodshed ensuing. Each rejection the writers experienced helped to eliminate such strange plot points from the screenplay.

The only studio that did not reject the concept outright was DreamWorks, the company responsible for producing *Old School* and the first studio Ferrell and McKay had approached. As it turned out, the success of *Old School* prompted DreamWorks executives to give the story a second look since Ferrell had become a box office star. Other studios began to reconsider, but the writers resubmitted their idea to DreamWorks. "This insane [process] was worthwhile in a way," says McKay, "because we wrote it so many times and it got tighter and better. And we landed at the right studio. They were the ones who were happy to have us."[59]

The Legend of Ron Burgundy

McKay was set to direct the screenplay, with Ferrell playing the lead role. Although the original draft had centered on a woman making her way in an all-male TV newsroom, after many rewrites, the emphasis had shifted to a male newsman who has to contend with workplace changes that were occurring in the United States in the 1970s. The script still contained a fair amount of bizarre and silly humor, but the filmmakers hoped audiences would find Ferrell's character palatable enough to anchor the plot.

Ferrell embodied Ron Burgundy, named after a type of wine that was very popular in the 1970s. His character wore a polyester blazer, had an overstyled hairdo and mustache, and held court among a coterie of fellow newsmen just as chauvinistic as Burgundy. Actress Christina Applegate played the new reporter, the first girl in the tree fort. Smaller roles went to such Ferrell film stalwarts as Vince Vaughn, Luke Wilson, and Ben Stiller.

New Productions

Ferrell's career had gained so much momentum by the time filming was completed on *Anchorman: The Legend of Ron Burgundy* that even the lukewarm response to the release of *Starsky & Hutch* in February 2003 could not derail it. Now an established star in comedy films, Ferrell was about to experience an even more important event in his personal life.

Less than two weeks after the release of *Starsky & Hutch*, Will and Viveca Ferrell became the parents of a son, Magnus Paulin Ferrell, born on March 7, 2004. The first-time parents chose not to encourage media attention on their new son. "We didn't want to do a press release or anything,"[60] Ferrell jokes.

Summer Surprise

The impending release of *Anchorman* was almost as nerve-wracking for Ferrell as the anticipation of his son's birth. There was a lot riding on the film for Ferrell after the success of *Old School* and *Elf*. Having been accepted as a comedy film performer by audiences who had loved his portrayal of characters who were endearing, he was now challenged to transfer his unique brand of comedy into a character who was decidedly less likeable.

Frank "the Tank" Ricard, though far from a model citizen, had been a supporting character audiences could recognize and laugh at. Similarly, the character of Buddy, whose childlike enthusiasm was not unlike Craig, Ferrell's Spartan cheerleader character on SNL, quickly endeared himself to fans of the movie *Elf*. The response to *Anchorman* could not be predicted with certainty, since the story's silliness and the character's inherent unlikability were closer to Ferrell's earlier style of humor. Studio executives, however, were banking on another hit film from Ferrell, believing that Ron Burgundy's transformation during the course of the film would make him less repellent to audiences. Even so, Ferrell tried to keep the proper perspective about the effect the film's impending success or failure might have on his career: "I think some people put so much weight on it that it becomes overbearing. Hopefully you're creating stuff that will

Will Ferrell's *Elf* Helps a Toy Company

Almost as if it were a scene from the movie, Will Ferrell's *Elf* helped an established toy company regain its financial footing. In December 2003 *Newsday* writer Monty Phan illustrated the effect of placing a famous toy in a blockbuster movie. Here is part of his article, "Etch-a-Sketch Company Benefits from Movie Role."

> Shares of Ohio Art's stock are rising, and the only reason anyone could think of for the sudden jump was the movie *Elf*. An odd correlation, but a little background makes the connection clear: Ohio Art, based in Bryan, Ohio, makes the Etch A Sketch, which appears prominently in the movie *Elf*, the comedy starring Will Ferrell that's made more than $100 million thus far.
>
> At first, Ohio Art just supplied the toys themselves, including a dismantled version for use in a scene where elves assemble the Etch A Sketches. But in July, the company got a call from New Line saying the toy had a more prominent role—Ferrell's character uses it to make a "to do" list and to design a detailed version of "The Mona Lisa"—and worked with Ohio Art to create a campaign around the toy.
>
> Christopher Byrne, an independent toy consultant based in Manhattan, said that sales of the Etch A Sketch are "very strong" every year, so kids are aware of it. But it's the perception of the toy that's changed when used in a movie like *Elf*.
>
> "It's something that moms almost always buy because they think kids ought to have one," Byrne said. "Now it may be something that kids actually request. That's the difference."

make people laugh, but we're not changing world history–and now that I've said that, I'll probably be driving a UPS truck two years from now."[61]

The response to *Anchorman*, released on July 9, 2004, exceeded all expectations. The film, which had cost an estimated $26 million to produce, brought in more than $28 million at the box office on its opening weekend. Its total earnings through the summer exceeded $51 million, making the film an unqualified financial success. Ferrell's portrayal of hubris in comedic lead roles had clearly clicked with paying filmgoers.

Chapter 6

Will Power

THE SUCCESS OF *Anchorman* placed Ferrell in a rare and enviable position among film stars. He was allowed the freedom to pick and choose any project he wanted. As a name-above-the-title star, he was responsible for a film's failure or success, but now he was able to focus on finding projects that were perfectly suited to the niche he had carved for himself in film comedy. Almost a dozen such projects are already in various stages of production or awaiting release.

Working with Woody Allen

The next film Ferrell scheduled was known during production simply as *The Woody Allen Fall Project*. For any comic performer, working with Allen is a dream realized, and Ferrell was no exception. Woody Allen has been a major figure in American comedy since the early 1960s, first as a writer for the legendary TV sketch-comedy program *Your Show of Shows* with Sid Caesar, and later as a stand-up comedian in his own right.

Allen's greatest fame, however, has come from his work in films. As an actor, writer, and director of Academy Award–winning film comedies exploring romantic relationships, he remains a cult hero to fans around the world. His thinning red hair, prominent nose, and ever-present glasses helped create his persona of a sad little man, unlucky with women and at odds with the world. A personal scandal in recent years forced the reclusive Allen into the spotlight he had avoided for much of his career, but it did not diminish his work output of at least one film per year.

Allen originally wanted actor Robert Downey Jr. to play the male lead in the 2003 fall project. Unfortunately, Downey's drug-related problems made it difficult to get insurance, so Allen

Woody Allen works from the director's seat on the set of one of his films. The famed director cast Ferrell to play the lead role in his latest project, Melinda and Melinda.

decided to not hire him and looked elsewhere for a male lead. In the meantime, *Old School* proved to be a big hit, prompting Allen to contact Ferrell about the highly secret project. "Apparently Woody saw *Old School* and liked me," says Ferrell. "He sent me a script, which I had to send right back even after I'd said yes."[62]

The film, since named *Melinda and Melinda,* concerns two writers who tell the story of a woman's attempt to straighten out her life. A comedic version is followed by a tragic version. Ferrell played the woman's husband. When the film was in production in October 2003, he and the rest of the cast were not allowed to see the script in its entirety so the director could maintain the story's plot twist. What Ferrell was allowed to see of the script prompted him to do the film, but relating to the famously aloof writer/director proved difficult. "Woody Allen has been nothing but nice and complimentary to me, but every time I've tried to joke with him, I get nothing," Ferrell says. "He thanked me for doing the script and asked me if I liked it, and I said I really liked the car crashes. He went, 'Uh-huh. Anyway.'"[63]

Also in the cast was Steve Carell, who had worked with Ferrell on *Anchorman.* All he knew of his own role was that he would play Ferrell's best friend, who tries to talk him out of committing adultery. He was equally impressed with Allen but found not knowing the entire script to be a challenge. For Carell, the saving grace of working on the project was Ferrell. "One of the nicest guys, truly, that I've ever met," says Carell. "With him on set . . . you're going to laugh until you cry every day."[64]

The film premiered in September 2004 at the San Sebastian Film Festival in Spain to overall praise, and Allen received the festival's lifetime achievement award. Allen was asked at the festival how he came up with the name Melinda, and he gave a typical Allen response: "I chose the name Melinda because I type my scripts, and 'Melinda' is easy to type. It's the truth. All the names I use for my films are either very short, or easy to type."[65]

Kicking and Screaming

When his work on *Melinda and Melinda* was completed, Ferrell went directly into his next scheduled project. The film, called *Kicking and Screaming,* costarred seventy-year-old film veteran Robert Duvall and former NFL football coach Mike Ditka. The comedy centers around Ferrell's character, Phil Weston, who is the coach of his ten-year-old son's soccer team.

Going for the league championship, Phil's team is in direct competition with a team coached by his own father, Buck, played

Other Possibilities

Among the titles mentioned as possible upcoming films for Will Ferrell are several that were in the planning stages in early 2005. The most often mentioned are sequels to Ferrell's most successful endeavors, *Old School, Elf,* and *Anchorman: The Legend of Ron Burgundy.* Further possibilities include the following:

Fly on the Wall—A comedy about a down-on-his-luck lawyer whose life begins to improve after he innocently saves a fly from being swatted.

Stranger Than Fiction—An IRS auditor (played by Ferrell) begins to hear a voice in his head that seems to know everything about him, including when he will die.

Motorcycle Cop—A California Highway Patrol officer moves to L.A. because there's not enough crime in Irvine.

Marathon—A comedy about a man who proposes to his girlfriend at the start of a marathon. Ferrell told *Premiere* magazine: "She says no and the guy goes through the five stages of grief over 26 miles."

by Duvall. The two men, who both have ten-year-old sons and thirty-year-old wives, have been rivals for quite some time, and the championship game becomes a comedic test of wills.

Ditka plays himself in the film. Phil hires the onetime Chicago Bears coach to be his assistant, knowing that Ditka lives next door to Buck and that the two older men do not get along. Ferrell's ability to embody his character was in full form while making the movie. In one scene, Ditka shouts some standard words of encouragement to the players. Using a hesitant voice meant to suggest he has no idea what Ditka is talking about, Ferrell echoes the line: "Yes, Rome wasn't built in a day." With Ferrell's sense of comedic hubris, his character does not want to let on that he's unsure of the line's meaning, so without elaborating he tells his players, "Repeat it quietly to yourselves."[66]

Branching Out

By working at such an intense pace over a short period of time, Ferrell has gained considerable insight into the craft of acting over the course of his many projects. The discovery that audiences must come to like his characters before they will be prepared to laugh at his comedic efforts has been a valuable lesson. He has also been able to transfer his natural personal charm and warmth to the screen by playing characters of greater depth than the one-dimensional loonies represented by his previous roles.

His privileged position in the film industry has given him license to set lofty career goals that would have seemed impossible ten years ago. "My dream of all dreams would be to do what Tom Hanks and Jim Carrey have been able to do," he says, "make the transition somewhere down the line from doing comedy to dramatic parts in movies."[67]

He has already started the transition, first with the more "serious" Woody Allen comedy *Melinda and Melinda*, and then with a cameo appearance in a project called *Winter Passing*, a film about

With his role in Woody Allen's Melinda and Melinda, *Ferrell, seen here speaking with a journalist, has begun to take on more challenging roles.*

a young woman trying to reconcile with her reclusive father. Her return home is not a pleasant one as she encounters her estranged father in the company of an unusual assortment of characters. One of them is a shiftless musician, played by Ferrell as a wandering loner.

The independently made film was written and directed by playwright Adam Rapp. Ferrell managed to film his scenes in October 2003, in between work on his bigger-budget projects. "It definitely has comedy elements in it, but it's a somewhat serious drama," says Ferrell. "So I'm getting to do some really neat things in addition to the fun comedy roles. I couldn't feel luckier."[68]

Not Quite a Remake

Not all of Ferrell's upcoming projects are small-budget or independently made films. Of all the films Ferrell has been involved with recently, none has garnered as much attention as *Bewitched*, a major studio film due to be released in the summer of 2005. The comedy is partly based on a popular 1960s TV sitcom in which an advertising executive named Darrin Stephens unwittingly falls in love with and marries a witch named Samantha.

The TV show was immensely popular and has remained so for many years in syndication. However, the premise goes back much further than the TV series. The 1942 film *I Married a Witch* had a similar concept, as did the 1958 comedy *Bell, Book and Candle*, which was based on a popular stage play. What made *Bewitched* so successful was the inherent romantic comedy and the succession of semiregular guest-staring comedy veterans who played Samantha's strange relatives.

When the feature film version was announced, casting became a popular subject in chat rooms among fans awaiting news of which stars would play which parts. At first, Reese Witherspoon was considered for Samantha, but Nicole Kidman was eventually signed for the part. For the role of Darrin, Jim Carrey was the initial choice but various conflicts led to Ferrell landing the role.

Having learned his lesson from SNL spin-off films, Ferrell was not interested in doing the film if it proved to be just another remake of a popular TV show. What made him consider playing the part was the way in which the filmmakers approached the project. "I agreed to do *Bewitched* because [writer/director] Nora Ephron came up with such a unique twist," explains Ferrell. "I play Jack Wyatt, this fallen-from-grace film star who has had one too many recent flops. He's talked into doing a remake of *Bewitched* and true to the magic of Samantha the actors end up becoming part of the real family so I also play Darrin Stephens."[69] Ferrell and writing partner Adam Mc Kay also contributed to the screenplay.

An Overflowing Plate

When *Bewitched* completed filming, Ferrell's plate was still full. He lent his voice to the role of the Man in the Yellow Hat in the

Nicole Kidman appears opposite Ferrell in a scene from the upcoming film Bewitched, *an adaptation of the old television show.*

animated feature film *Curious George*, adapted from the popular children's story published in 1941 by H.A. and Margaret Rey. The inquisitive little monkey from Africa adopted by the patient and understanding Man in the Yellow Hat has been beloved by generations of American children. Ferrell's participation in the film clearly illustrates that he has not abandoned the genre of family films he ventured into with *Elf.*

Ferrell has also worked into his schedule small roles in films in conjunction with the previous costars dubbed the "Frat Pack." *Old School* costar Luke Wilson wrote a part for Ferrell in *The Wendell Baker Story*, a film Wilson also directed. Wilson is an ex-convict working in a retirement hotel and trying to get his life back together with the help of several of the hotel's elderly inhabitants. Wilson's brother, Owen, and Vaughn also cast Ferrell in their film *The Wedding Crashers*, a comedy about two men who try to take advantage of women at weddings. Both films had Ferrell appearing in high-profile, comedic cameos.

His appearance in these films are in keeping with Ferrell's overall view of his work. "Regardless of what I do in other areas, I'll always return to R-rated, goofy comedies," he explains. "I work with a lot of people who have that as their drumbeat. It's great to do different things, but I'll always come back to that."[70]

Writing His Own Ticket

Working in projects with like-minded filmmakers is just one of Ferrell's many working principles. He pursues his own self-generated projects as well, such as two screenplays he cowrote with *Anchorman* writing partner and director Adam McKay. *Talladega Nights* and *August Blowout* have been in development for several years and may or may not ever see the light of day as finished films.

The project that seems the most likely to be produced is *Talladega Nights*. The comedy takes place in the world of high-speed sports car racing, with Ferrell playing a race car driver. McKay and Ferrell sold their screenplay to Columbia Pictures for $4 million, but as 2004 drew to a close no date had been set to begin production.

The other project is moving even more slowly. *August Blowout* is a comedy about an Orange County car salesman, desperate to

Ferrell poses with an award he received at the 2001 American Comedy Awards. The actor admits that he will always return to comic roles.

meet his monthly quota, who will stop at nothing to ensure success. The script was purchased by Paramount Pictures in April 1999 but has been in limbo ever since.

Sherry Lansing, the head of Paramount Studios, let Ferrell and McKay know that in no uncertain terms she did not care for their script. Over the next four years the two men rewrote the script fifteen times. "Everyone was thinking that if we just changed something, she'd [accept] it," says McKay. "To her credit, she was always on record that she didn't like the script."[71]

The Curse of Ignatius

While it is possible that both *Talladega Nights* and *August Blowout* will one day be produced, just as *Anchorman* was, another project dear to Ferrell's heart also remains in limbo. The project is a film version of *A Confederacy of Dunces*, the Pulitzer prize-winning novel by the late John Kennedy Toole. The title of the project comes from the writings of Jonathan Swift: "When a true genius appears in the world, you may know him by this sign, that the dunces are all in confederacy against him."[72]

The plot of *Dunces* centers around Ignatius J. Reilly, a corpulent intellectual who lives in New Orleans with his strange mother in 1963. In a tale that does not easily lend itself to summarization, Reilly comments on the world around him as he avoids work and verbally abuses his mother. Toole's manuscript was rejected repeatedly by publishers during his lifetime, but the author's mother persisted, and in 1980 the book was published. The Pulitzer prize was awarded posthumously.

Over the next two decades many attempts were made to turn the cult novel into a film. Comedians John Belushi, John Candy, and Chris Farley were all mentioned as likely candidates to play Ignatius but each one died shortly after his name was announced. This unusual series of fatalities, following the untimely death of the author, has led some to believe that the project is cursed.

Ferrell, a fan of the novel since his college days, is not one who believes in the curse. His name has been attached to the project since 2003, after several different studios, producers, and directors all attempted and eventually abandoned the project. Buoyed by the prospect of Ferrell's involvement, a production schedule, cast, and crew have been assembled more than once. Recently, however, just before filming was to begin, the project was again abandoned, this time due to lack of financing. "*A Confederacy of Dunces* is looking back in limbo," says Ferrell. "It's the movie that everyone in Hollywood wants to make but doesn't want to finance. They don't see it as a lucrative endeavor, but I think that movie just has to be made for the sake of making it. It's easier for me to say because I don't have to worry about paying the money."[73]

Musical Debut

Yet another highly anticipated project to which Ferrell's name has been attached is the film version of the very successful Broadway musical *The Producers*. Like *Dunces*, the project has had a very colorful history. It first appeared in 1968 as a comedy film written and directed by comedy legend Mel Brooks, who won an Oscar for best original screenplay.

Tsunami Relief Concert

The tsunami that devastated Southeast Asia in December 2004 generated a record amount of emergency charity relief. In spite of his busy work schedule, Will Ferrell found time to lend his name and talent to the relief effort by appearing at a three-hour benefit concert held in Los Angeles on January 17, 2005.

The concert featured several major rock acts, with Ferrell introducing the performers as well as appearing onstage throughout the show. The big-name acts included Eddie Vedder, Beck, Dave Grohl, and Joshua Homme, with Ferrell providing backup cowbell for the performers—as he had done on a popular SNL sketch. Comedian Chris Rock also provided a brief monologue between the music performers.

The acoustic concert headliner was the two-man rock act known as Tenacious D, consisting of actor/comedian Jack Black and Kyle Gass. The duo played several classic rock tunes and was joined onstage for the finale by the other performers, including Ferrell, with his ever-present cowbell. The money raised from the concert was given to the American Red Cross Relief effort.

The Producers is the story of a wily Broadway producer named Max Bialystock who convinces Leo Bloom, a naive accountant, to join him in a scheme to bilk elderly investors out of their money. They plan to use the money people foolishly give them to produce a musical so awful it can only flop, allowing the partners in crime to keep the investors' money. The musical they choose, *Springtime for Hitler*, written by a crazed ex-Nazi named Franz Liebkind, is so bad it becomes a hit as an unintentional comedy.

The black comedy has become a cult hit over the years and helped launch the film career of Brooks, who, like Woody Allen, is an icon of American comedy. Brooks made several extremely popular film satires in the 1970s, but his last several projects were less successful. His career was resurrected in 2001 when he turned *The Producers* into a Broadway musical, which set a record for the most Tony Awards ever won by a Broadway musical.

The film will star Nathan Lane and Matthew Broderick, recreating their Broadway roles as Bialystock and Bloom. Ferrell is set to make his singing and dancing debut as the deranged Nazi

With the ability to play both comic and serious roles, Will Ferrell has a very bright future ahead of him.

playwright Liebkind. "I haven't seen a script yet so I don't know how true the film will follow the play," says Ferrell. "I do know they want me to sing at least one song. I am so happy Mel Brooks signed me up before he heard me sing."[74]

The project has stalled on several occasions due to scheduling conflicts. Lane delayed filming when he took over the role for a touring company in England. Nicole Kidman, cast as the curvaceous secretary, bowed out when the delay necessitated by Lane's commitment caused a conflict with the start of a project she was to star in with Russell Crowe. The film went into production in 2005, with Ferrell very much hoping that no schedule conflicts will prevent him from working with Brooks, the director of such classic film satires as the 1974 releases *Blazing Saddles* and *Young Frankenstein.*

A Bright Future

Ferrell will definitely be seen on the big screen over the next few years, although perhaps not in all the projects his name has been associated with. Fans of his brand of outrageousness and comedic hubris can anticipate seeing him in several high-profile projects. As for now, "I'm just keeping my eye on what's directly ahead," Ferrell says, "and that's all I can really worry about."[75]

His screen persona established, Ferrell is capable of moving in any direction, from romantic leads to the occasional drama. Armed with the knowledge of what sustains a successful film career and a fan base willing to see him expand within his persona, Will Ferrell can look forward to a bright future.

Notes

Chapter 1: One Happy Little Boy

1. Quoted in Louis B. Hobson, "Will Power," *Calgary Sun*, October 16, 1999, p. E 10.

2. Quoted in Scott Raab, "Behind the Sophomoric Slapstick Lie a Misunderstood Comic Genius, an Underappreciated Thespian Brilliance, an Introspective Soul Striving to . . . Oh, Never Mind. The Dude Is Funny, All Right?" *Esquire*, December 12, 2003, p. 129.

3. Quoted in Dan Jewel, "Night Moves," *People Weekly*, April 6, 1998, p. 143.

4. Quoted in Mal Vincent, "SNL Alumnus Reaches New Heights in Elf," *Virginian-Pilot*. November 7, 2003.

5. Quoted in Rebecca Murray, "Will Ferrell Finds His Inner Elf," *Romantic Movies*, October 2003. www.romanticmovies.com.

6. Quoted in Liz Braun, "Will Ferrell Making Fame for Himself," *Toronto Sun*, November 2, 2003.

7. Quoted in Katie Couric, "Will Ferrell Takes on TV News," *Dateline* transcript, MSNBC.com, June 25, 2004. www.msnbc.msn.com/id/5296084/.

8. Quoted in Rob Blackwelder, "So Elfin' Funny," *SPLICEDwire*, October 23, 2003. www.splicedwire.com/03features/ferrellfavreau.html.

9. Quoted in Hobson, "Will Power," p. E 10.

10. Quoted in Indiana Sev, "An *Elf* Made Man: joblo.com Interviews *Elf* Star Will Ferrell," joblo.com, November 7, 2003. www.joblo.com/index.php?id=2842.

11. Quoted in Marc Peyser, "Comedian in Chief," *Newsweek*, February 19, 2001, p. 56.

Chapter 2: A Funnyman's Groundwork

12. Quoted in Sam Jones, "Wild Will Ferrell," *Premiere*, November 2003, p. 93.

13. Quoted in Heather Wadowski, "Back to School with Class Clown Will Ferrell," http://univercity.com/march03/willferrell.html.

14. Quoted in David Rensin, "20 Questions with Will Ferrell," *Playboy*, November 2001, p. 123.

15. Quoted in Hobson, "Will Power," p. E 10.

16. Quoted in Jennifer Armstrong et al., "Will Ferrell: Movies, The Must List," *Entertainment Weekly*, June 25, 2004, p. 93.

17. Quoted in Lee Shoquist, "Will Ferrell: Elf Role, Big Talent," Reel Movie Critic.com, 2003. www.reelmoviecritic.com/20038q/id1985.htm.

18. Quoted in Jones, "Wild Will Ferrell," p. 93.

19. Quoted in Shoquist, "Will Ferrell: Elf Role, Big Talent."

20. Quoted in Rensin, "20 Questions with Will Ferrell," p. 124.

21. Quoted in Blackwelder, "So Elfin' Funny."

22. Quoted in Tom Shales and James Andrew Miller, *Live from New York: An Uncensored History of* Saturday Night Live. Boston: Little, Brown, 2002, p. 547.

Chapter 3: The Best Utility Man in Comedy

23. Quoted in Shales and Miller, *Live from New York*, p. 446.

24. Ken Tucker, "Saturday Night Live," *Entertainment Weekly*, October 13, 1995, p. 62.

25. Quoted in Shales and Miller, *Live from New York*, p. 465.

26. Quoted in Couric, "Will Ferrell Takes on TV News."

27. Quoted in Resnin, "20 Questions with Will Ferrell," p. 124.

28. Quoted in John Jeremiah Sullivan, "Comedy Is Pretty," *GQ*, July 2004, p. 100.

29. Quoted in David Wild, "Looking for the Heart of Saturday Night," *Rolling Stone*, November 27, 1997, p. 54.

30. Quoted in Peyser, "Comedian in Chief," p. 56.
31. Quoted in Braun, "Will Ferrell Making Fame for Himself."
32. Quoted in Jewel, "Night Moves," p. 143.
33. Quoted in Shales and Miller, *Live from New York*, p. 481.
34. Quoted in Raab, "Behind the Sophomoric Slapstick," p. 129.

Chapter 4: Small Screen to Big Screen

35. Quoted in *The Ladies Man*, Paramount Home Video, 2000.
36. Quoted in *The Ladies Man*.
37. Quoted in Shales and Miller, *Live from New York*, p. 481.
38. Quoted in Resnin, "20 Questions with Will Ferrell," p. 124.
39. Quoted in Sullivan, "Comedy Is Pretty," p. 101.
40. Quoted in Jones, "Wild Will Ferrell," p. 94.
41. Quoted in Dennis Hensley, "From Bush to Camp," *Advocate*, September 11, 2001, p. 41.
42. Quoted in Julian Roman, "An Interview with Director Will Ferrell," Latino Review.com, December 2003. www.latinoreview.com/films_2003/newline/elf/will-interview.html.
43. Quoted in Shales and Miller, *Live from New York*, p. 508.
44. Quoted in Shales and Miller, *Live from New York*, p. 506.
45. Quoted in Jeff Jensen, "Will He or Won't He?" *Entertainment Weekly*, February 28, 2003, p. 32.
46. Quoted in Jensen, "Will He or Won't He?" p. 33.
47. Quoted in Jensen, "Will He or Won't He?" p. 34.

Chapter 5: Breaking Through on Film

48. Quoted in Wadowski, "Back to School with Class Clown Will Ferrell."
49. Quoted in Sullivan, "Comedy Is Pretty," p. 156.
50. Quoted in Shoquist, "Elf Role, Big Talent."
51. Quoted in Matt Soergel, "Everything Came Together for 'Elf' Writer," *Florida Times-Union*, December 5, 2003.
52. Quoted in *Elf*, New Line Home Video, 2004.

53. Quoted in *Elf.*

54. Quoted in *Elf.*

55. Quoted in Roman, "An Interview with Director Will Ferrell."

56. Quoted in Joe Neumaier, "The Biggest Dope in Hollywood," *New York Daily News,* July 4, 2004, p. 2.

57. Quoted in Dan Snierson, "Jack Black & Will Ferrell: Class Clowns, Entertainer of the Year Ranking," *Entertainment Weekly,* December 26, 2003, p. 40.

58. Quoted in Robert Abele, "On the Set: News Hounds," *Premiere,* July/August 2004, p. 63.

59. Quoted in Dana Harris and Claude Brodesser, "Films Buried Alive," *Variety,* June 21, 2004 p. 1.

60. Quoted in Rabb, "Behind the Sophomoric Slapstick," p. 130.

61. Quoted in Rabb, "Behind the Sophomoric Slapstick," p. 130.

Chapter 6: Will Power

62. Quoted in Louis B. Hobson, "Will Ferrell Joins Woody Movie," *Calgary Sun,* October 26, 2003.

63. Quoted in Joel Stein, "Big Time: Will Ferrell Takes Spastic Exuberance to the Movies," *Time,* November 10, 2003, p. 90.

64. Quoted in Hanh Nguyen, "Comedian Comments on Anchoring, Adultery," zap2it.com, December 16, 2003. www.zap2it.com/movies/news/pstory/0,3382,19825,00.html.

65. Quoted in David Michael, "The Woodman Woes San Sebastian," *stew.com,* September 30, 2004, p. 2.

66. Quoted in Sullivan, "Comedy Is Pretty," p. 156.

67. Quoted in Shales and Miller, *Live from New York,* p. 517.

68. Quoted in Christy Grosz, "Comedy Star of the Year," *Hollywood Reporter,* September 26, 2003, p. 4.

69. Quoted in Louis B. Hobson, "All About Will Power," *Calgary Sun,* July 8, 2004 p. E-11.

70. Quoted in Neumaier, "The Biggest Dope in Hollywood," p. 2.

71. Quoted in Harris and Brodesser, "Films Buried Alive," p. 1.

72. Quoted in Chris Faile, "InSCRIPTions Screenplay Review: 'A Confederacy of Dunces,'" FilmJerk.com, December 26, 2002. www.filmjerk.com/new/article374.html.

73. Quoted in Shoquist, "Will Ferrell: Elf Role, Big Talent."

74. Quoted in Hobson, "All About Will Power," p. E-11.

75. Quoted in Joshua Rich, "Elf to Neo: Buh-Bye!" *Entertainment Weekly*, November 28, 2003, p. 17.

Important Dates in the Life of Will Ferrell

1967
John William Ferrell is born on July 16 in Irvine, California.
1975
Parents Lee and Kay Ferrell divorce. Will and younger brother, Patrick, split their time between both parents.
1990
Graduates from USC with a degree in sports information.
1991
Joins the Groundlings, an improvisational comedy troupe in Los Angeles.
1995
Joins the cast of *Saturday Night Live* with several other Groundlings veterans.
1997
Makes big-screen debut in *Austin Powers: International Man of Mystery*.
1998
Cowrites and stars in SNL spin-off film *A Night at the Roxbury*.
1999
Appears in SNL spin-off film *Superstar*, plays reporter Bob Woodward in Watergate-era film parody *Dick*, and reprises role in *Austin Powers: The Spy Who Shagged Me*.
2000
Marries Viveca Paulin. Appears in *Drowning Mona* and in SNL spin-off film *The Ladies Man*.

2001
Stars in short-lived animated TV series *The Oblongs*. Appears in the films *Zoolander* and *Jay and Silent Bob Strike Back*. Becomes one of the highest-paid cast member in the history of SNL ($350,000 per year) and receives an Emmy nomination for his work on SNL.

2002
Leaves SNL after seven years to pursue a full-time film career.

2003
Appears in the hit films *Old School* and *Elf.*

2004
Son Magnus Paulin Ferrell is born on March 7. Has a cameo in the film *Starsky & Hutch*. Cowrites and stars in *Anchorman: The Legend of Ron Burgundy*.

2005
Stars in *Melinda and Melinda, Kicking and Screaming,* and *Bewitched.* Provides voice for the Man in the Yellow Hat in *Curious George,* and begins filming the musical *The Producers.* Makes cameo appearances in *Winter Passing, The Wedding Crashers,* and *The Wendell Baker Story.*

For Further Reading

Books

Leonard Maltin, *TV Movies and Video Guide.* New York: New American Library, 1989. An excellent reference tool for film or TV scholars and enthusiasts. The author and his team of editors meticulously researched thousands of films and TV movies, annually updating film titles, running times, year of release, major cast, and other pertinent data in alphabetical listings.

Tom Shales and James Andrew Miller, *Live from New York: An Uncensored History of* Saturday Night Live. Boston: Little, Brown, 2002. Very well-written chronicle of the metamorphosis of SNL, with many anecdotes from the participants of the show up to the present day. Includes interviews with virtually every cast member and writer, including Ferrell. A must-read for any fan of the show.

Jeffrey Sweet, *Something Wonderful Right Away.* New York: Limelight Editions, 1987. The only known book detailing the fascinating history of improvisational comedy theater in America, this book contains interviews with many of the pioneering figures, including Ben Stiller's parents, Anne Meara and Jerry Stiller, and original SNL cast member Gilda Radner.

Web Sites

City of Irvine (http://www.ci.irvine.ca.us).
Excellent source for the history, statistics, and events concerning Will Ferrell's hometown. Includes many links to such other sites as Ferrell's alma mater, University High School.

The Groundling Web Site (http://www.groundlings.com). Official website for the comedy troupe that includes information on their history, classes, ongoing shows, and ticket information. The photo album includes information on such famous alumni as Will Ferrell and other now famous cast members.

Internet Movie Database (www.imdb.com/name/nm0002071). Includes a biography of Ferrell as well as pictures, external Web site links, details of his films, and daily updates of his projects.

Planet Will: The Will Ferrell Web Site (planetwilljt.org). Fan-based Web site with much to recommend in terms of imaginative graphics and interesting text and move site links. Also includes information on Ferrell's costars, including Chris Kattan and Cheri Oteri. Unfortunately, it is not updated often, so much of the information is out of date.

Saturday Night Live **Web Site** (http://snl.jt.org). Anyone seeking information on the history of *Saturday Night Live* will find it here. Every episode, every host, every musical guest, every sketch, and every character are meticulously categorized. Even lists everyone who ever opened the show with the famous line. Important to read homepage instructions before continuing, otherwise it can be very confusing.

Works Consulted

Periodicals

Robert Abele, "On the Set: News Hounds," *Premiere*, July/August 2004.

Steve Appleford, "Lords of Thunder: At the Wiltern, Tenacious D and Pals Bring the Rock to Help Victims of the Wave," *City Beat*, January 26, 2005.

Jennifer Armstrong et al., "Will Ferrell: Movies, The Must List," *Entertainment Weekly*, June 25, 2004.

Bret Begun, "Where There's a Will, There's a Way to Laugh," *Newsweek*, February 24, 2003.

Scott Bowles, "'Anchorman' Will: Film at 11" *USA Today*, July 6, 2004.

Liz Braun, "Will Ferrell Making Fame for Himself," *Toronto Sun*, November 2, 2003.

Christy Grosz, "Comedy Star of the Year," *Hollywood Reporter*, September 26, 2003.

Dana Harris and Claude Brodesser, "Buried Alive," *Variety*, June 21, 2004.

Dennis Hensley, "From Bush to Camp," *Advocate*, September 11, 2001.

Louis B. Hobson, "Will Power," *Calgary Sun*, October 16, 1999.

——, "Will Ferrell Joins Woody Movie," *Calgary Sun*, October 26, 2003.

——, "All About Will Power," *Calgary Sun*, July 8, 2004.

Jeff Jensen, "Will He or Won't He?" *Entertainment Weekly*, February 28, 2003.

Dan Jewel, "Night Moves," *People Weekly*, April 6, 1998.

Sam Jones, "Wild Will Ferrell," *Premiere*, November 2003.

William Keck, "'Anchorman' Makes News," *USA Today*, June 30, 2004.

——, "On Nuns, Star Wars, & Evil Designers," *Esquire*, August 1, 2001.

Rebecca Murray, "Will Ferrell Finds His Inner Elf," *Romantic Movies*, October 2003.

Joe Neumaier, "The Biggest Dope in Hollywood," *New York Daily News*, July 4, 2004.

Marc Peyser, "Comedian in Chief," *Newsweek*, February 19, 2001.

——, "Al and Dubya After Hours," *Newsweek*, October 30, 2000.

Scott Raab, "Behind the Sophomoric Slapstick Lie a Misunderstood Comic Genius, an Underappreciated Thespian Brilliance, an Introspective Soul Striving to . . . Oh, Never Mind. The Dude Is Funny, All Right?" *Esquire*, December 12, 2003.

David Rensin, "20 Questions with Will Ferrell," *Playboy*, November 2001.

Patty Rhule, "Will Ferrell Proves His Star Power," *USA Today*, July 12, 2004.

Joshua Rich, "Elf to Neo: Buh-Bye!" *Entertainment Weekly*, November 28, 2003.

Sean Smith, "The Art of Idiocy," *Newsweek*, July 12, 2003.

Dan Snierson, "Jack Black & Will Ferrell: Class Clowns, Entertainer of the Year Ranking," *Entertainment Weekly*, December 26, 2003.

Gabriel Snyder, "DVDs Spawn a New Star System," *Variety*, May 31, 2004.

Matt Soergel, "Everything Came Together for 'Elf' Writer," *Florida Times-Union*, December 5, 2003.

Joel Stein, "Big Time: Will Ferrell Takes Spastic Exuberence to the Movies," *Time*, November 10, 2003.

John Jeremiah Sullivan, "Comedy Is Pretty," *GQ* July 2004.

Ken Tucker, "Saturday Night Live," *Entertainment Weekly*, October 13, 1995.

Mal Vincent, "SNL Alumnus Reaches New Heights in Elf," *Virginian-Pilot*, November 7, 2003.

David Wild, "Looking for the Heart of Saturday Night" *Rolling Stone*, November 27, 1997.

Internet Sources

Rob Blackwelder, "So Elfin' Funny," *SPLICEDwire*, October 23, 2003. www.splicedwire.com/03features/ferrellfareau .html.

Katie Couric, "Will Ferrell Takes on TV News," *Dateline* transcript, MSNBC.com, June 25, 2004. www.msnbc.msn.com/id/ 5296089/.

Chris Faile, "InSCRIPTions Screenplay Review: 'A Confederacy of Dunces,'" FilmJerk.com, December 26, 2002. www. filmjerk.com/new/article374.html.

David Michael, "The Woodman Woes San Sebastian," www .filmstew.com/Content/Article.asp?Contentid=9792&pg-1.

Hanh Nguyen, "Comedian Comments on Anchoring, Adultery," zap2it.com, December 16, 2003. www.zap2it.com/movies/ news/story/0,1259,--19825,00.html.

Julian Roman, "An Interview with Director Will Ferrell," Latino Review.com, December 2003. www.latinoreview.com/ films_2003/newline/elf/will-interview.html.

Indiana Sev, "An *Elf* Made Man: joblo.com Interviews *Elf* Star Will Ferrell," joblo.com, November 7, 2003. www.joblo.com/ index.php?id=2842.

Lee Shoquist, "Will Ferrell: Elf Role, Big Talent," Reel Movie Critic .com, 2003. www.reelmoviecritic.com/20038q/id1985. htm.

Heather Wadowski, "Back to School with Class Clown Will Ferrell," http://univercity-com/march03/willfarrell.html.

DVDs

The Concert for New York City, Columbia Music Video, 2001.

Elf, New Line Home Video, 2004.

The Ladies Man, Paramount Home Video, 2000.

Saturday Night Live: The Best of Will Ferrell, Volumes 1 & 2, Lion's Gate Home Entertainment, 2002.

Index

Picture Credits

About the Author

Dwayne Epstein was born in Brooklyn, New York, and grew up in Southern California. His first professional writing credit was in 1982, writing film reviews and year-end analysis of popular culture.

Nationally, he has been a regular contributor to several film magazines since 1996. Internationally, he contributed to Bill Krohn's *Serious Pleasures* in 1997, which saw publication in Europe. Epstein has had several children's books published since 2000 and is currently writing a biography of actor Lee Marvin. Epstein also authored *People in the News: Adam Sandler* and *History Makers: Lawmen of the Old West*, both for Lucent Books. He lives in Long Beach, California, with his girlfriend, Barbara, and too many books on movie history.